# OPENING TO HEAL

Shepherd Hoodwin

Summerjoy Press
LAGUNA NIGUEL, CALIFORNIA

OPENING TO HEALING

Summerjoy Press
99 Pearl
Laguna Niguel CA 92677-4818

shoodwin@gmail.com
https://shepherdhoodwin.com

Copyright © 2014, 2020 by Shepherd Hoodwin

All rights reserved. No part of this publication may be reproduced, stored in a retrieval system, or transmitted, in any form or by any means, electronic, mechanical, photocopying, recording, or otherwise, without the prior written permission of the publisher, except by a reviewer, who may quote brief passages in a review.

ISBN: 9798652700263; Kindle: 978-1-885469-16-8

Photograph of Shepherd Hoodwin by John Kilis.

Dedicated to

*The beautiful soul who was*

**Susan Rubenstein Weiss**

# ACKNOWLEDGMENTS

My clients, for their questions and the use of session material.

Leslie-Anne Skolnik, Pat Kendall, Stan Grindstaff, Dave Gregg, Lucy Anderton, Ellen Fauerbach, Fiona Camberun, Kathryn Schwenger, and Kathy Lew, for editing.

Linda Scheurle, Flo Nakamura, Fay Goldie, Seth Cohn, Barry Carl, Kent Babcock, Patricia Englert, Patte LeVan, Ed Hamerstrom, and J. Jones, for transcribing.

# CONTENTS

ACKNOWLEDGMENTS — iv
PREFACE — viii
   MICHAEL CHANNELING — x
   ORGANIZATION — xi
   EDITING — xii
INTRODUCTION — xiii

## I FINDING YOUR POWER — 1
1 • FORCE — 2
2 • PERSONAL POWER — 13
3 • ENERGY MANAGEMENT — 19
4 • ACCEPTANCE AND SOLVING PROBLEMS — 24
5 • BALANCE AND HEALING — 32

## II THE NATURE OF ENERGY — 40
6 • RELEASING BLOCKS — 41
7 • MOVEMENT — 43
8 • BEING CONSTRUCTIVE — 45
9 • WORKING WITH ENERGY — 48
   THE FUNDAMENTAL ELEMENT — 48
   NEGATIVE ENERGY — 48
   THE MOST DIRECT ROUTE — 49
   HELPING — 49
   WORKSHOPS — 50
   ENERGY AS LOVE — 50
10 • ECSTASY — 51

## III HEALING PRACTICE — 56
### 11 • HEALING OTHERS — 57
- OFFERING — 57
- FREEDOM FROM LIMITATION — 57
- HEALING ENVIRONMENT — 58
- INTUITION — 58
- INTENT — 58
- ABILITY TO HEAL OTHERS — 59
- HEALING RITUAL — 59
- APPROACHES TO HEALING — 59
- HEALING IS RECIPROCAL — 60

### 12 • THE MEDICAL ESTABLISHMENT — 61
### 13 • HOW BLOCKED EMOTIONS FEEL — 63
### 14 • ENERGIES IN THE BODY — 65
### 15 • CHAKRAS — 69
### 16 • CRYSTALS AND GEMSTONES — 73
### 17 • NUTRITION FOR THE ILL — 78
### 18 • HEALING AFFIRMATIONS — 80

## IV BECOMING WELL — 95
### 19 • PURGING — 96
### 20 • RECOVERING — 103
- MOTIVATION — 103
- BELIEFS — 103
- DISCOMFORT — 103
- CHANGING BODY CONSCIOUSNESS — 104
- SLEEP — 104
- BURNOUT — 104

## CONTENTS

| | |
|---|---|
| IMBALANCE | 104 |
| 21 • REBALANCING | 105 |
| 22 • FINDING A REASON TO LIVE | 108 |
| 23 • CHANGING THE BODY'S IMPRINT | 110 |
| 24 • HEALING YOURSELF | 114 |
|     ONE HUNDRED PERCENT COMMITMENT | 114 |
|     RESPONSIBILITY FOR LIVING | 116 |
|     THE PERFECT PATTERN | 116 |
|     THE PURPOSE OF ILLNESS | 117 |
|     THE NATURE OF HEALING | 117 |
|     DOING THE WORK | 118 |
|     LEVELS OF SELF | 122 |
|     TRUST | 122 |
|     LETTING GO | 124 |
|     YOU ALREADY HAVE THE POWER | 127 |
| 25 • RAISING YOUR VIBRATION | 128 |
| 26 • WELL-BEING IS YOUR BIRTHRIGHT | 130 |
| 27 • THE FLOW OF HEALING | 131 |
| **BACK MATTER** | **133** |
|     ABOUT THE AUTHOR | 134 |
|     GLOSSARY | 136 |
|     OTHER BOOKS BY SHEPHERD HOODWIN | 137 |
|     REVIEWS | 141 |

# PREFACE

Everything is energy. What we experience as solid is simply a particular frequency of energy. Our bodies are the surface manifestations of far more extensive energies. To ignore form is unwise, but to ignore the energies behind form is to disregard most of what is. We can all learn to discern energy. People experience energy in many different ways—there is no one right way.

This book is not focused on physical techniques, nor is it an in-depth study of mental or emotional factors in illness—many good books are already available on those topics. Rather, it focuses on the spiritual: in particular, it is an exploration of energy and its impact on our lives, particularly with regard to healing. We are all on a path of healing, and being aware of energy can help us experience greater well-being in everyday life. However, it is especially relevant to those who are dealing with illness in themselves or others.

There are many causes of illness. Working with spiritual, emotional, and mental factors can only support the healing process, but some illnesses are caused by genetic or environmental influences, poor diet, accidents, and other hazards of the physical plane. It should not be assumed that if someone is sick, it is his fault—this only places the added burden of guilt on him. Two illnesses that appear similar can have quite different causes, and there is rarely just one factor behind an illness. Many spiritually oriented people take a simplistic view and jump to conclusions. We do create our own reality, but that doesn't necessarily imply that if a person is sick, he created the illness out of a limiting belief or stuck negative emotion, although that can be the case.

Taking responsibility is vital, and looking at how we may have helped create our present circumstances is useful. Taking responsibility, however, is primarily about choosing

## PREFACE

to create healing now. Opening to healing and doing whatever we can physically, emotionally, mentally, and spiritually will bring the highest possible outcome. That may or may not include bringing the physical body to full functionality, but whatever happens, the journey is worthwhile. If a person begins this journey when her body is beyond repair, she can still reduce her pain, create greater peace of mind, and help heal her soul. We are eternal beings, and no growth or lessons are wasted.

    I underwent Lasik eye surgery in 1997. Only recently had corneal surgeons been able to operate on people with myopia as extreme as mine, and it was still a challenge for them. Before, during, and after the surgery, I focused on opening to healing. I affirmed that spirit was guiding the surgeon to work perfectly, to bring forth the highest possible result. I also affirmed that I was receiving guidance to cooperate perfectly with the process. Beforehand, I had asked several friends to send me energy, and even people I hadn't asked told me later that they were inexplicably thinking about me around the time of the surgery. During the procedure, I brought my awareness to my eyes and let them soften in receptivity to love and light. Afterward, I affirmed that I was totally in spirit's hands and that all was well.

    Following the surgery, the doctor sent me to my hotel room to sleep for a couple of hours, and then I was brought back to his office so that he could check my eyes. He was astonished: three hours after the surgery, the cornea had completely healed, something he'd never seen before. The next morning when he measured my eyesight, the results could not have been more ideal. Later, I told him that I had worked with opening to healing energy. He replied, "I believe it!"

    Another story: Once, when I was in a car accident, I knew I wasn't seriously injured, but there was some whiplash and I was in shock. While I was waiting for the police and ambulance to arrive, I gathered my wits as best I could and said to myself, "Well, I'm writing a book about opening to healing. I guess this would be a good time to do that." I started affirming, "I am well. The universe is healing me. ..." Each time I did, I started crying, but I was also calmly observing myself cry. The tears were cleansing away trauma, and felt good. I continued this as I lay on my back in the emergency room, waiting interminably for the radiologist to come. After X-rays had been taken and it was confirmed that I had no broken bones, I walked home. I was still somewhat dazed, but knew that healing had begun.

In both these experiences, I didn't feel anything mystical or transcendent—I couldn't particularly feel the energy, and wondered at the time if anything was happening. However, I kept my intent focused on opening to the highest possible energy, and that was sufficient. My goal is to live in this state of relaxed openness all the time.

Your experience of this book can itself be an opening to healing. I suggest that you read slowly and meditatively, relaxing into the spirit of the words.

I accessed the material in this book through channeling, working with a nonphysical entity known as Michael. In my work with Michael, I have become keenly aware of the importance of energy. Over the years, they gradually expanded my capacity to channel not only their words but also their energy, so that now, the energetic aspect of my channeling is as important as the words. Almost everyone feels at least some energetic upliftment when I channel. Many feel that the energy work we do has a significant impact on their lives.

Before reading the channeled material, you might find some background helpful.

## MICHAEL CHANNELING

Channeling is a process of allowing a nonphysical

# PREFACE

intelligence to express through a person who is the "channel." It can be in words, energy, emotion, movement, and/or music, among other things. Michael is the name of a group or "entity" of 1,050 individual souls who have completed the physical and astral planes of creation, and teach from the causal plane. This is why they refer to themselves as "we." (They are not the same as the archangel Michael.) There are several Michael books by a number of other channels and authors who work with this same Michael group.

Most of the other Michael books deal with the Michael teachings, a complex and fascinating body of information about the way we set up our lives. *Journey of Your Soul: A Channel Explores the Michael Teachings* is my contribution thus far to that body of information. *Opening to Healing*, like *Loving from Your Soul* and the other books in this series, does not cover the technical aspects of the Michael teachings, although it illuminates many of its principles. The few terms associated with the teachings are defined in the glossary.

## ORGANIZATION

More than half the material in this book comes from lectures. The rest is from individual sessions. Some of the chapters are compilations of passages from various lectures and sessions. Most of those passages are in their own subchapter. If there are two or more different passages in a single subchapter, they are separated by asterisks. Questions and comments are italicized. Some chapters contain material that was originally directed to a specific person, yet is potentially useful to others. Unless implied by subtitles or questions, these are noted under the chapter title: *To a Specific Individual*, etc.

## EDITING

When I channel, Michael makes use of the contents of my consciousness, and to some degree is limited by my limitations. Although this material is well beyond what I could produce on my own, it is also mine, and I take full responsibility for it. In general, I treated the original transcripts like first drafts, and polished them as I would my own writing, cutting, rearranging, and rewriting as necessary. Before publication I channeled Michael to get their modifications and "stamp of approval."

*Opening to Healing* presupposes that we are each a soul who has lived other lives, but believing in reincarnation or even in channeling is not necessary for an enjoyable and profitable reading experience. You can validate most of the ideas in it for yourself, and Michael encourages you to do so.

Sessions with Michael are themselves healing, as well as clarifying and uplifting. May you experience this as you read their words.

> Shepherd Hoodwin
> Laguna Niguel, California
> June 21, 2020

# INTRODUCTION

To heal fully, there must be an acknowledgment of that which is not whole. If you are apparently physically healthy but ignorant of the empty places in you beneath the surface, you probably will not remain physically healthy. Like a building on a foundation with gaps that in time collapses, your body is susceptible to the forces of destruction to a greater extent than if you have been lovingly allowing the empty places beneath the surface to fill in. Although health of the physical body is a blessing and is important, the physical body itself is only a small part of the picture. Even mental and emotional health are not central to health. There is no real health without spiritual, or energetic, health. That is why this collection of discussions on opening to healing has been assembled.

It is difficult to attain the body's true potential for physical health—or even what passes for health today—in the world the way it is. Pollution of all kinds conspires to weaken the body's natural healing mechanisms. However, the challenges of living in the world as it is can cause you to heal in more profound ways and free your spirit. A working knowledge of energy is a valuable tool for transforming first yourself, and then the world around you.

We would encourage you to feel the energies of the words as you read this book, so you may be lifted into an experience of them.

Michael

# Part I

# FINDING YOUR POWER

# 1 • FORCE

An essential quality of the universe is dynamic power, which fuels all that occurs in it. Without power, there would be stagnation. This power springs from the Tao—the All That Is. You might envision a vast power station, "Tao Power & Light," with cables extending from it out into the universe. The universe is a construct of the Tao, and the Tao powers it through these "cables." Everything is hooked up, or it could not exist, including you. Your power comes through your connection to the Tao.

If a toaster has a bad cord, the cord resists the flow of electricity, creating heat within itself instead of in the toaster. Likewise, a person's resistance to the flow of power creates excess heat. When you are releasing the blocks and distortions that resist the flow of power in you, you sometimes experience them more keenly rather than less, because you are no longer ignoring them. When you have completed letting go of them, however, greater power moves through you, bringing increased fulfillment, pleasure, and aliveness.

When power moves freely and fully, it tends to bring health. When it moves freely and fully on the level of the physical body, it tends to bring physical health. However, human beings are obviously not merely physical bodies; you have emotional, intellectual, and spiritual bodies that affect your physical body. When power moves freely and fully through all levels of self, true health is possible.

Letting power move in such a way that healing occurs is an art and science. Universal power has innate intelligence, but wholly manifesting that intelligence requires mature perception and understanding. Letting go of blocks is essential, but there is more to manifesting universal power than "getting out of its way"—you must be able to move with it. When you move with it on all levels of your being—physical, emotional, intellectual, and especially, spiritual—you manifest your force. Your force is your substance as a person—your birthright, you might say. The *Star Wars* movies popularized the phrase "May the Force be with you." In fact, you are the Force. Those who feel it necessary to force others or themselves to do or be something do not know that they are the true force. One of the purposes of spiritual studies is to acquaint you with your own force. The more you know it, the less dependent you are on outside sources. We are not speaking here of forcefulness; someone who exudes authority is not necessarily manifesting his force.

Why is it that most people are not familiar with their force? Many people fear it. As force passes through the personality, it magnifies distortions and pushes against blocks. If you wish to let go of what "clogs the pipes" of your force, you welcome the intensity of its experience. False personality (ego), however, tends to resist an increased experience of force. We are not browbeating false personality. It is, after all, present for a reason; it has played its part in the development of everyone on the physical plane. But there is a time and place for everything.

If you are aware that false personality is interfering with the expression of your force, find out what it is afraid of losing and assure it that you will look after its concerns. It may fear that if it is not in control, you will not survive. (It views itself as an expert at protecting you.) You can then tell it all you are doing to ensure your survival, and that you will not accept more force than you can safely handle.

It is usually best to move one step at a time. Some people tap into their force without much preparation and have a destructive experience because it brings out what is destructive within them more quickly than they can handle. The fable about the tortoise and the hare applies: if you work on one block at a time and increase your acceptance of your force in small increments, you will more quickly reach the goal of fully manifesting it than if you try to do it all at once. In such a progression, there is more grace and less wasted motion.

When you are bathed in force externally, through a channel, healer, in group meditation, or whatever, it calls from you your own force—like attracts like. As you begin to resonate with this external force, you generate a harmonious atmosphere in which your own force can come forth. As with all things, however, this can be overdone. You could go several times a week to someone who channels energy, and would thereby experience an intensification of force, but after a certain point, you would likely find this unbalancing. If you are listening to yourself, you will know when you are ready for another "dose" of external force.

Sometimes healers say that they do not heal you; rather, they draw forth from you your own healing currents. This is often true, but occasionally the healer's force does do the healing. If that is the case, the client may not be able to sustain the healing unless he eventually allows his own force to come forth, at least in the specific area of illness. At times, however, the healer's force is adequate to heal the condition permanently even without him realizing his own force, especially if he does not have strong resistance.

Force, as we are using the term here, is more than what is commonly called life force. Life force is the part of your force that your physical body manifests. You can project it in self-defense, for example, creating a field around your body; even animals do this. Perhaps we can call the overall force "spiritual force" to distinguish it from life force, since the spiritual level of self, being the highest, encompasses the intellectual, emotional, and physical levels; it expresses your wholeness. If you offer life force to someone in a healing way, it is like recharging his body's battery. Spiritual force, however, can be healing physically, emotionally, mentally, and spiritually—it affects a larger portion of the person than life force alone.

There are those, particularly among younger people, who have a strong life force but relatively little spiritual force, because they do not yet have the emotional, mental, and spiritual development to sustain it. There are also those, particularly among older people, who are frail physically but have a relatively strong spiritual force; enough universal power is manifesting in their bodies to support its manifestation, but the physical aspect of their force is proportionately minor. Your force is most potent when all four levels are adequately developed and strong, although each person has a different mix—some people naturally emphasize intellectual expression of force, for example, while in others, the purely spiritual is more dominant.

*Are healers tapping into their own force, or some other universal source?*

Many healers channel energy in addition to their own force. If you wish to heal someone and are not yet manifesting adequate force to do the job, you can ask that another source assist you.

Ultimately, all force comes from the Tao, so if a healer says that it is coming from God, he is correct. It does not matter whether the force is coming solely through his own cable connected to Tao Power & Light, or it is routed first through other beings or energies to amplify the current.

*If the channel or healer is carrying personality distortions or energy blocks, can he transmit them to the client, like a virus?*

Generally not, provided that his primary intent in offering healing is loving. If he does not adequately put them aside, they simply stop or distort the flow of force, so that it does not have the desired effect. The force may magnify the distortions, but any damage that occurs is likely to be done to the healer, not to the client. The client may feel that the atmosphere is not quite right, but unless his own distortions and blocks resonate sympathetically with the healer's, the client's essence usually just shuts him down, limiting the inflow of energy.

*But like does attract like. Isn't resonance one of the reasons that someone seeking healing chooses a particular healer from the array of healers available?*

Yes, but not necessarily resonance with distortions and blocks. In the example above, it could be that the healer is usually able to put aside distortions adequately to do the job, but on this particular day he is not. Perhaps the client has had good experiences with this healer in the past. You cannot generalize too much about such things.

It is true that in some cases a person is attracted not only to the force but to the distortions in a healer. This gives them both an opportunity to work on their distortions. It is not necessarily inappropriate. It is just not going to be healing, at least not in the way expected.

*Could you name some things that a person whose force is flowing freely and clearly would typically be doing other than healing?*

Such a person could be doing anything. If he is working in a nine-to-five job, he would have ease and contentment in it if that is what is appropriate for him to be doing. Everyone has a different capacity for manifesting force, in terms of both quantity and quality, so what is appropriate is also different. When your force flows freely at the quantity and quality that are now natural to you, without blocks and distortions in its way, whatever you do has a higher level of effectiveness with less friction or wasted energy than the same action with more resistance and, consequently, less force.

The quantity of force relates to presence: the more force you manifest, the more others tend to notice you. The quality of force relates to its intensity, depth, and refinement. A person who is allowing his force to flow freely and abundantly may still be manifesting a less refined quality of force than someone who is not. An actor or politician, for instance, known for having charisma may manifest much force, but the force is not necessarily of a refined quality. On the other hand, a spiritual teacher known for his healing presence may manifest both a high quality and quantity of force.

Also, a true spiritual teacher is likely to strongly manifest his force on a spiritual level, as well as physically, mentally and emotionally, whereas the actor or politician's force may be more limited to the physical. Of course, there is no reason an actor or politician cannot have a refined, balanced force, and there is no guarantee that a spiritual teacher's force will be refined and balanced. Sometimes, those on a spiritual path lack physical or emotional development, for instance.

Although someone must have a certain level of life force to support a high level of spiritual force, his life force may not be particularly strong compared to that of an athlete, for example. Life force to some degree depends on physical health, strength, and vitality. Those with a strong life force but not a strong spiritual force also tend to have a noticeable presence, but it is not as expansive as the presence of those with a strong spiritual force, since it also includes the emotional, mental, and especially, spiritual, which is the most expansive aspect of self.

*Does manifesting your force depend on being conscious of it?*

It is helpful to know consciously that you are your force, so that you can deliberately open to it. It is not so much a matter of being conscious of the force itself, however, as of being conscious in what you do so that your force can flow into it. To make an analogy, you do not give much thought to the electricity involved in cooking a meal. You cook the meal and the electricity is there, supplied in the proper amounts because the appliances are already plugged in. The point is to be plugged in.

Consciousness of the blocks and distortions resisting your force may be necessary in order to release them. Through practices such as meditation, you can increase your consciousness in general, as well as expand your capacity for force. However, if you are letting your force flow freely into whatever you are doing, your capacity will naturally tend to expand.

As mentioned, a person needs to have a certain amount of life force to provide stability for the manifestation of spiritual force, but most people are capable of more spiritual force at their present level of life force than they are manifesting. Also, the body's capability to handle spiritual force can be stretched, depending on its "elasticity." For these reasons, people with about the same amount of life force may have widely differing amounts of spiritual force. If someone is in ill health, his body's energy tends to pull inward to try to deal with its problems. In that case, his body may not be very "elastic," and increasing his spiritual force beyond a certain point can be harmful. Still, if he has much unused capacity for force, which is the case for most people, he can take advantage of it without taxing his body much. An increase up to that point is beneficial for his health, and gentle stretching beyond that may also be. It is overstretching that can be damaging. Even in a healthy person, stretching this capacity is not always a comfortable process, and sometimes it leaves him tired. It is like stretching in physical exercise: respecting the body's limits and gently taking it slightly beyond them when appropriate is beneficial, but forcing the body to stretch is harmful. A healthy person can generally expand her limits more quickly than a sick person can, but most people can expand their limits to some extent.

A person's life force potential grows from birth fairly steadily until around the age of thirty. It remains about the same for a while, and then begins to decline. The timing of the decline depends on how well he takes care of himself physically, and his mental, emotional, and spiritual state. It is possible to maintain your life force with little diminution for quite some time—thirty, even forty, years. But in this society, the decrease begins around the age of forty for most people. In any case, if you allow it to, your spiritual force can keep increasing when your life force stabilizes and even decreases.

In addition to your body, your environment is a factor in how much force you manifest. If you are inhabiting a highly troubled place, an excessive increase of force would intensify the problems. There must be a space beyond you capable of receiving it. This really does not relate to your own capabilities, but you may not be able to use your capabilities fully under highly stressful or troubled circumstances.

Your capability to manifest force is primarily a function of the specific nature of your essence. Each person is unique, having had his own pattern of experiences over eons dealing with force. In addition, some people are more attracted to working with higher intensities of force than others. It is not better to manifest higher rather than lower quantities of force. It is useful for there to be a variety in this regard. Someone whose life is low-key may not want to manifest as much force as someone more prominent—a lot of force might attract more attention than he wants, or there may be no place for it to move. If you are spending a lifetime as a monk, for example, a relatively low or moderate level of force is probably comfortable. Most people could benefit from some increase in force, but there is not a contest to see who can manifest the greatest amount. The point is to release your blocks and distortions so that you can manifest the force natural to you in your situation.

*I thought of an analogy: one person is like a watch at 1.5 volts; another, a transistor radio at 9 volts; another, an electrical appliance at 120 volts; and so forth. Each person is right for where he is, and nobody could take his place.*

To continue that analogy, if you put a 10,000 volt generator in your watch, you would not have a watch very long!

*Is one of our problems that we compete with each other to have more force?*

We do not think that most people are even aware of force, in the way we are discussing it. Certainly those who engage in power struggles are not. Perhaps there are a few in spiritual circles who feel competitive about it, but this is probably not a major problem on Earth today.

*Doesn't force fluctuate?*

Yes. It fluctuates based on the need of the moment. For example, the force coming through this channel is far greater when he is channeling than when he is washing dishes. When he is washing dishes, there would be no place to go for the power he experiences while channeling. It would likely just stay in his body and damage it. Also, there are variations when channeling. There is more force during a group session where there is responsiveness to the force than during an individual session where there is the same level of responsiveness. Also, some people have greater capacity to receive force than others, so among individual sessions, there is variety. One person with a high native capacity for force who is relatively free from blocks and distortions might draw more from the channel than a small group would. With another person, it might not be safe for very much force to come through.

*Can we use force coming through a channel or healer to get rid of the blocks and distortions within us?*

As you are bathed in force, it puts pressure on them, giving you a greater opportunity to recognize them and let them go. However, you must take responsibility for the process. Passively bathing in force does not alone remove blocks.

You do not process all blocks and distortions consciously. You must process them on some level, though, integrating their lessons, to release them. They are there for good reasons. Receiving lessons from your blocks and distortions is an important means of growth. If you tackle too many at once, you will feel overwhelmed—you can only grow so much at a time—but most people are not taxing their capacity in this regard.

*It seems that we can no longer afford to take our time doing this.*

Those who excessively retard or postpone letting go of their blocks and distortions are going to have their hands full. On the other hand, as there is greater force manifesting on the planet, processing can occur more easily and quickly. What would have taken a year to process ten years ago might take six months now. In ten more years it might take a month, if there is willingness. Because the speed will have increased gradually, most people will not notice the difference very much.

*Are we going to see more "miracle cures" resulting from people quickly releasing blocks that they've been holding for years?*

Yes. When blocks and distortions are released, symptoms that sprang from them begin to heal. When that happens quickly, it is sometimes called a "miracle." A cure is valid and "miraculous," though, whether it happens quickly or gradually.

## MEDITATION

Go within and feel your own force. Allow it to push out any distortions or blocks ready to move. Sense how freely your force moves in you. Speak to it, welcoming it more fully into you. Ask that your force be integrated into your life as fully as possible.

## 2 • PERSONAL POWER

What makes you individually powerful? You are powerful, you know. You are so powerful that you were able to materialize yourself where you are right now. You might think that is nothing; you do it all the time. Nonetheless, it is quite remarkable: you decide to go somewhere, and bingo, you are there! You have to travel to get there, perhaps in a vehicle of some kind, but you do usually get there. In fact, you materialized yourself in a physical body on this planet in this solar system in this universe. You did that! No one else did it for you. That is pretty remarkable, is it not? You also manage to create the experiences you are having in your life. That is no small task. If you are not using your personal power in the most deliberate and constructive manner possible, you can learn how.

Name an area in which you would like to manifest your power more constructively.

*Physical healing.*

How would you go about using your personal power to bring physical healing? Particularly if someone is of a New Age orientation and believes that he is responsible for his health, he may feel frustrated if he cannot do something about it as quickly or easily as he would like. He may criticize himself because of this. "There must be something wrong with me. Maybe I am spiritually defective. Otherwise I would not have this health condition." That is not necessarily the case; there are many possible reasons for a health condition. A strong soul may handicap her life game to give herself additional challenges. If you chose especially difficult ones, maybe you were a little cocky! Some people think that they were under the influence of alcohol when they set up their life—we assure you that this was not the case!

In bringing your personal power to bear on a situation, detachment is important. It can be difficult to detach when you have pain, but it is helpful to take stock objectively of all the facts. You might start by listing all your symptoms. Include when they arise, and what you have tried doing about them as well as what you have not. Then, name your feelings: "I feel guilty for being sick." "I enjoy the attention I'm getting." "I feel frustrated by my lack of success in dealing with this." And so on.

Review the approaches you have tried: What helped? What did not? Maybe certain steps helped, but you stopped doing them. You may have just forgotten about them, such as a certain exercise—those can be easily forgotten! Consider what you have not tried. Do any of them speak to you? For example, if you have a sense that you are dealing with a past-life issue, have you tried past-life regression to see if you can get more knowledge about it?

There is much power in acceptance. Work to accept your condition as part of your game plan for this life rather than seeing it as an inconvenience preventing you from doing what you want to do. If you had a past-life issue that you wanted to be sure to deal with, you may have put it into your body; by dealing with your physical symptoms, you are also dealing with the issue. The fact that you were able to manifest your condition shows how powerful you are. When you accept your condition, you are better able to bring your power directly to bear on it and perhaps be more effective in changing it.

Be aware of the parts of your body that are working well and give thanks for them. Notice them as you are walking down the street: "My knees are working well. Thank you." If they were not, you would certainly notice them, but it seems unfair to notice your knees only when they do not work well. Celebrate your body and any enjoyment it gives you, even though parts of it are not functioning quite the way you would like.

Your body may be telling you about emotional blocks through a physical problem. By unblocking them, not only do you feel better physically and emotionally, but you are better able to join emotionally with others. You might not have had the motivation to deal with those emotional issues if you had not had the physical problems. Your ailments might also motivate you to explore your spiritual dimension more fully. If that brings an awareness of yourself as an ongoing, everlasting being, you might see your ailment as a small price to have paid. You might also find that in seeking help for your condition, you meet some wonderful people whom you would not have met otherwise.

You apply your personal power by saying, "I am the source of my life. Therefore, I can seek solutions. I can use my creativity to find ways of dealing with this." If you have a blind spot preventing you from thinking of the most effective solution, that might be why you have the physical problem to begin with. Seeking to bring yourself out of that blind spot can be a catalyst for spiritual awakening.

The more confidence you have in your power, the more effectively you will use it. Sometimes people with physical ailments think of themselves as being victims of them. If nothing they have tried has worked, they could easily draw the conclusion that nothing will work. Usually, though, it is only an indication that they have not yet tried what will work. Sometimes it does take much patience.

However, there are cases in which, in a practical sense, nothing can be done. Usually these are repayments of karmic debts. Truly incurable diseases account for only a small part of all cases of ill health. Most situations can be improved or completely changed.

In what other area would you like to apply your personal power more constructively?

*Financial security.*

The issues relating to financial security are similar to those relating to health. Many people are passive in their use of personal power to create financial security. They believe that they are victims and that there is not much they can do about it. "After all, the politicians control everything. ... It's who you know. ... It's easy for them—they were born with it." And so forth. Although some people are born into money, if you go back far enough in their families, somebody started with nothing except his own personal power. If those who inherit wealth do not have an adequate sense of personal power, they are likely to squander it.

As with health, when you allow your creativity to come up with appropriate, workable ideas for generating money and you fully realize them, financial success will usually follow. Manifesting personal power is largely a matter of moving forward. If you do not know what to do, pick the best idea you can think of and move forward with it. If you are in movement, a better idea will come to you, but if you are stuck, your "juices" are not flowing and your power is not expressing through you.

This is what goal setting is about. Goals are merely a trick to get you to move forward. It is not really so important that you reach the specific goals you set for yourself. Very often they change before you reach them—that is all right. The point is not the target but your enjoyment of the constructive expression of your personal power.

Megalomaniacs, people who love the power to control other people, are usually lacking in self-esteem and a sense of their own personal power. If you think you need the power of money, authority, a booming voice, or an imposing body to have power, you do not know your personal power. Personal power is the power of your love, acceptance, and passion. Even if you were locked in a prison, chained to a wall, if you discovered your personal power, you would be set free. Maybe you would not be set physically free, at least not immediately, but your soul would be set free. After exploring every possible way of dealing with that situation, if there was no external way out, your soul might find freedom through death. That is a different experience than dying as a victim.

No external force has true power over a free person. In religion, figures such as Jesus are often thought of as having been victims, but that was not the case. They knew their personal power. Others could not truly harm them. In spite of whatever those others did to them physically, their creativity was great enough to handle it.

There is a saying that you are never given something you cannot handle. That is not always true. Sometimes you really are not equipped to handle what comes along. In that case, you can express your power by leaving the situation, if that is possible. In a sense, leaving is a way of handling it. In any case, you are free if you are fully exercising your personal power in whatever ways are available to you. That is something you are here to learn how to do.

*What about abused children?*

If you are incarnating into a potentially abusive circumstance, you usually know that beforehand. There are several possible reasons you might choose such a circumstance. Once in a while it is a karmic repayment. Often a person accepts abuse as part of the "package" because he needs that particular body and the people he will meet through it to complete his life plan. Sometimes people deliberately choose abusive circumstances for growth, or to give the gift of love and compassion to the abusers—children often have a remarkable way of continuing to love adults who do terrible things to them. This can have a radical impact on the abusers, even if they do not recognize it consciously at the time. Finally, sometimes the abuse is not chosen at all but is the result of unforeseen circumstances.

A child's personal power is limited, and usually cannot eliminate abuse. In fact, there are always limits on how much you can influence external events, but such limits are greater for a child. Nevertheless, he brings his personal power to bear in the choices he makes in handling abuse. Later in life, he can bring it to bear in the actions he may take to heal his wounds. A mature adult freely and fully manifesting his personal power, which is the power of love, can have tremendous impact on the world. This can be seen in people such as Jesus. The point, though, is not your impact on the world, but the creative expression of your power. Even if that does not change circumstances, it changes your experience of them.

## 3 • ENERGY MANAGEMENT

Managing your personal energy is an important skill. When you arise in the morning "on the wrong side of the bed," you have an opportunity to practice energy management, especially if you felt well the preceding night. Why is your energy field now full of debris? You might say, "I didn't sleep well last night." Why didn't you sleep well last night? It probably relates to cleansing. Cleansing occurs on all levels—emotional, mental, and spiritual as well as physical. Of course, eating heavily before bed could result in your waking up feeling poorly. The reason is that digestive wastes are circulating in your blood—your body is trying to eliminate them. Once they are out of your system, you usually feel better.

What about emotional debris? Perhaps you had a nightmare. You tossed and turned, and woke up feeling terrible. Again, if you ate heavily before bed, that may have been a factor, since the body, mind, emotions, and spirit are all connected. A nightmare, though, is usually your psyche trying to digest something emotionally heavy. It may have been in your emotional "stomach" for a long time. Now you are trying to break it up and move it out. You may temporarily feel worse than if you had just left it there. Once it is fully out of your system, however, you will feel lighter and emotionally freer.

Likewise, perhaps you have been intellectually unresolved about an issue that is bothering you. You slept poorly because you were working to digest or integrate an experience. When you complete that, you feel better.

What is most relevant to this discussion is the spiritual, or purely energetic, level. If you are carrying stuck or stagnant spiritual energy, you may have been trying to release that in your sleep. (Of course, you do not have to wait for sleep to release inner debris. You can let it happen consciously.) Again, each level of self influences the others, and each is important. However, the spiritual level, being the subtlest, is the most frequently overlooked. It is also the most influential, in a sense, because it is the atmosphere in which the three other levels operate.

Health on any level requires free, unblocked movement. The nature of energy is to move. As Einstein lucidly explained, matter is also energy, so the nature of matter is also to move. Your body needs to move to be healthy. If somebody is sick in bed, it is often helpful for him to get up and walk regularly if he can, going slightly beyond his comfort level, in order to expand his capacity for movement. Intellect and emotion are also forms of energy and require movement. Crying is a form of emotional movement—it is common knowledge that a good cry can be healing not only emotionally but physically. You can promote intellectual movement by freely exchanging ideas and being willing to let your understanding grow and change. You can also learn to discern and allow spiritual movement.

Being stuck cannot be sustained. Eventually, everything must move. The state of no movement at all is death, but at death, movement occurs on other levels. The essence is freed to do other things, and the body sooner or later breaks down and participates in other growth processes.

Just as too little movement can result in poor health, so can too much movement. Some people damage their bodies through excessive physical exercise or simply going all the time without adequate rest. Likewise, some burn out intellectually or emotionally by frenetic movement on those levels. There is a balance of rest and action that brings health. Energy seeks movement, but it moves from a place of rest. Rest and movement are a polarity to be balanced and unified. Either one in separation from the other is detrimental.

Managing your energies includes your physical, mental, emotional, and spiritual energies. Let's go back to the example of waking up on the wrong side of the bed. If you have not yet learned mastery of your energies, you may stay in a bad mood all day long. This means that the emotional debris that has been freed as a result of the movement initiated in a nightmare, for example, is in limbo in your emotional body. It has not yet moved all the way out, and it cannot go back where it was. It is just sitting there until your emotional body somehow processes it out and heals the part of itself that held it. Your emotional body will eventually heal itself—like the physical body, it tends to be self-healing. However, if you are skilled in energy management, you know how to finish the job quickly and comfortably so you can move on to something else.

Sometimes people unconsciously deal with what was stirred up emotionally overnight, at least partially, while taking a hot shower, or during a quasi-religious ritual, such as drinking a cup of coffee at the altar of the breakfast table. Nevertheless, processing without conscious participation is generally slower and less effective. If you focus on what is releasing, identify it, and do what is necessary to complete the process, it can be over relatively quickly.

Likewise, if your spiritual body has been releasing toxins, a brief meditation could move out that debris. Perhaps overnight you also left your body and visited people who needed healing. You may have taken on some of their energies, and now you need to move them out so they can dissipate. If you identify with the energies you have taken on, you will bring them more deeply into your aura and fasten them there, creating a problem you did not have before.

Have you ever had the experience of suddenly feeling miserable, and assigning the source of that misery to someone in your vicinity who made an innocent remark? Maybe you picked a fight, and then had some additional debris to handle. If a feeling, thought, or sensation suddenly comes to you, stop for a moment and try to identify its true source—such feelings are not always your own. They can be messages. See if a picture comes to mind. You might think of someone you had not thought of in a while. You might want to call that person. Whether they are your feelings or not, the way to deal skillfully with them is the same: identify and heal them as well as you can and allow them to move. If you try to push them out before you heal them, they may come back as though connected to you on a retractable cord.

*Is there a way to reduce the pain of emotional release without stopping it?*

Release should be a mostly pleasing experience. You may simply need to find greater surrender to the process. It is important not to judge or edit what is occurring. Let yourself cry, rage, or whatever in a safe place. Choosing a safe place is part of loving yourself. You would only choose to release in an unsafe place as an act of self-hatred. If there is a safe place, let it happen.

You may be trying to release too much at once, or maybe you need help from your friends, either on or off the physical plane, or from a therapist of some kind.

There are parts of the food you eat that are useful as nutrition or energy, either stored in your body or used immediately. Other parts are waste insofar as you are concerned, although they are useful to the earth as fertilizer. Likewise, there are parts of your experiences that provide growth, and parts that are waste. Suppose that you have a good discussion with someone. He presents his point of view, and you present yours. As you digest what you have shared, you take from it what is useful to you and get rid of the rest. However, if points of disagreement are stuck in your mind, going around and around and not getting out, you have mental waste that burdens you until it is released.

When you have trauma, by definition you have taken on an experience that you are not able to handle. Everyone has experienced trauma, in other lifetimes if not this one. There are lessons in trauma, but at first they are incompletely digested. When you are in a healing phase later, you go back and finish digesting them. You empty so you can refill with new "food." In other words, you make room for going on and having new, more productive experiences.

*When trauma manifests physically, such as in chronic constipation, how do you go about healing it?*

Working on all levels is helpful. Physically speaking, dietary changes, colonic therapy, herbal and fiber cleansing programs, bodywork, and so on, may be useful. Also, explore what you are not eliminating emotionally from your gut. See if you have a thought that goes around in your mind like a subliminal mantra, such as "I'm stuck here," manifesting in your body. Moving spiritual energy can help get everything else moving, so you may want to look at practices such as meditation and visualization.

*How can you recognize past-life emotions that are still weighing you down?*

You could try a meditation in which you visualize a doorway leading to an emotion you are ready to release. When you walk through it, you may find yourself in a past lifetime in which that emotion began to form or was increased. You might also find yourself moving into the emotion directly, without past life recall. In either case, explore what arises.

# 4 • ACCEPTANCE AND SOLVING PROBLEMS

Transitions are often not easy. Physical illness can give evidence of an important transition. You could compare the physical body's suspension of activity during illness to going into neutral to shift gears in a car. Normally, a car's gears are engaged in a set pattern. The purpose of going into neutral is to allow a new arrangement to occur. If everything is set, resistant to change, going into higher gear is not possible.

Of course, you do not have to become physically ill to end old patterns and begin new ones, and there are many other possible reasons for illness. It is common among New Age people to see illness as a failure of some kind. This is not necessarily the case. How many human beings, including the most enlightened spiritual people, are never sick? Even those who go for years without manifesting symptoms may not be functioning at optimal health. Illness is one of the lessons of the physical plane. It is neither good nor bad; it is something to handle when it comes up. It gives you many opportunities to make specific kinds of choices, not only in terms of what to do about it, but in terms of your attitude about it.

Because of the fear of death, illness usually brings forth many emotional currents. If you do not fear death, you are likely to have an easier time with illness because you are not resisting it so much. The resistance to illness sourced in resistance to death may be deeply buried and therefore not accessible to conscious awareness. In such a case, it is a weight you feel but take for granted without identifying it. As a result, it might appear that you accept your illness, but this may not be the fact. If you accept your illness, you feel that whatever happens is all right. If you apparently become sicker, that is all right. If you develop painful symptoms, that is all right. If you die, that is all right.

We are not suggesting that you deny your body's natural

## ACCEPTANCE AND SOLVING PROBLEMS

drive to survive, and we are not recommending that you take actions that lead to death. You have gone to a lot of trouble to be here on the physical plane, and one of the lessons of the physical plane is to care for your body properly. What we are saying is that when you are ill, if you have done everything you can physically, mentally, emotionally, and spiritually, you can let go, with the attitude that whatever happens, happens.

Part of the proper care of your body may be going to health practitioners who know more about specific methods of treatment than you do. There are two ways you can approach this. You can go as most people do, out of fear, asking to be healed by forces outside of yourself. Or you can go motivated by love, love for your body, with interest in learning what you can from the experience. In partnership with the health practitioners, you can seek better ways to care for your body.

The source of anxiety is a lack of acceptance. True acceptance contains two elements in balance with one another. The first is the attitude that things are perfect exactly as they are. The other is making choices, based on how things are, that can improve your situation.

How can it be said that things are perfect exactly the way they are if you are sick? Your life is primarily the result of your prior choices. Others have impact on your life, for both good and ill, but you are the primary source in your life. You chose your body and basic life situation. In addition, you make ongoing choices about how you live your life, including how you care for your body. So your life reflects your choices.

If you are a painter, you can step back from your canvas and evaluate what you see. Whether you like what you see or not, you have learned something. You now know what happens when you combine particular pigments in a particular way. It is not a wasted experience. Knowing that you created it, you can change it.

Although being sick is obviously not pleasant, it may actually be bringing you to a higher level of health and well-being. It may be cleansing toxic substances from your body through fevers, coughing, or whatever.

Let's look at another, larger issue: the shamefully large number of people starving. How can it be said that things are perfect as they are for them? We are not suggesting that there isn't great room for improvement. However, current reality is a perfect starting point. It is an opportunity to exert your own power to bring change. Since starvation is created collectively by all humanity, it can be uncreated if humanity so chooses. By stating that things are perfect as they are in the face of problems such as illness or starvation, you are letting go of self-defeating angst. If you truly understand what you are saying, you are not ignoring the problems; you are coming to peace within yourself about them. As long as you are on the physical plane, there will be problems to solve. If you do not accept this, you are continually in turmoil and do not enjoy life. Acceptance brings equilibrium and strength from which you can create new realities. If you are deeply concerned about world hunger and accept current reality as it is, you have more energy to devote to solving the problem than if you are in conflict about it. If you do not have acceptance, you are likely to judge those who appear to be causing the problem. This is likely to increase conflict rather than aiding you in helping to solve it.

We are not suggesting that you close your eyes to political or other factors that might be contributing to the problem. However, the more neutral you are about what you see or think you see, the better able you are to be a constructive force for change. The more inner peace you have, the more clearheaded you are likely to be in recognizing what can actually be done to solve problems.

Acceptance is the key to love. Where there is no acceptance, there is no love. The person who is truly

## ACCEPTANCE AND SOLVING PROBLEMS

accepting is not a doormat or a wimp with no backbone. If, in the name of acceptance, someone is unwilling to take constructive action to change situations, he only understands the first half of acceptance. Activism is not everyone's path. If someone, however, has the attitude that nothing should be done because, after all, things are perfect the way they are, he misunderstands acceptance. That can result in a lack of compassion.

For example, some take the attitude that those who are starving chose to be born in that situation or created it; therefore, they must live with it. If you were living in a house that caught on fire, you would not feel it would be appropriate for the fire department to say, "Well, you created that situation; you will have to put the fire out yourself." That certainly would not be a loving attitude. We are all in this together, and we include those of us who are nonphysical in that statement.

You cannot act on every problem you see. You might view the problems of the world as being like the "help wanted" ads—you cannot go to work for all the firms who advertise. It is important that you sense what your path is, where you can be of the highest benefit to yourself and others. Healing yourself is as much a contribution to the whole as healing others, since you are part of the whole. Any act motivated by love, which is the intent that the highest good be served, is an invaluable contribution to the whole. What you specifically do is not that important. If you are in that neutral place of acceptance, you will be clear on what your highest path is.

Your thoughts can be a significant contribution. Unrealized thoughts are incomplete, but you do not necessarily have to be the one who realizes your thoughts for them to be effective. Sending loving thoughts to those suffering from hunger is not providing food, yet it can be an impetus for others who are in a position to provide food. No loving thought is wasted. Of course, if you are also able to provide something concrete, so much the better.

*Sometimes apparently loving thoughts mask anger or other not-so-loving feelings. For example, if my body is sick, and I feel angry and frustrated about it, adopting a loving thought might be a denial of how I'm feeling.*

You can take a loving approach both to your body and to your anger and frustration at being sick. You can see your physical and emotional states as being perfect the way they are—both give you starting points for healing. The illness of your body is a starting point for healing your body. The anger and frustration in your emotions are starting points for healing your emotions. If you do not consciously choose to constructively influence what is occurring in your body and emotions, you are leaving what happens to chance or to automatic processes. You will simply continue to be frustrated and angry until some other feeling happens to come along. That diverts energy from healing.

If you do not accept yourself, you probably do not think that you are perfect as you are. Everything in the universe has room for expansion. Otherwise we would not have much to do. This does not mean, however, that things are not perfect as they are.

Children prosper when you unconditionally accept them. They mature faster and learn more easily. Judging them hinders change. It is like building a concrete wall around them defining them. Likewise, when you judge yourself, you freeze yourself into a pattern that is difficult to change. When you acknowledge your perfection, it is much easier to love yourself. In fact, loving yourself occurs because you acknowledge that you are perfect as you are. The statement that you are perfect as you are suggests that you deserve unconditional love. If you feel that you are imperfect as you are, you believe that there are parts of yourself that are not worthy of love. You therefore withhold love and

## ACCEPTANCE AND SOLVING PROBLEMS

acceptance from yourself. Without love and acceptance, you cannot grow or change as quickly as you could with it, so it is a catch-22.

*It's one thing to say, "I am perfect as I am. I love myself." It's another to feel it. How do you get the feeling?*

The thought usually comes first. Without it, you are not likely to have the feeling. Then you can bring your other thoughts in line with it. Suppose that you repeat the affirmation, "I am perfect as I am." Then five minutes later, you stub your toe and say, "I'm a stupid idiot for stubbing my toe." Your second affirmation is obviously in conflict with the first and neutralizes it. As you bring all your thoughts in line with the positive affirmation, you can imprint it into your consciousness. This takes being awake and noticing your thoughts. For example, if you hear yourself calling yourself stupid, you can remind yourself that it is all right to stub your toe sometimes, and that you are perfect as you are. As you act toward yourself in a conscious, loving way, you become more aware of emotions not in agreement with your new thoughts, such as feelings of inadequacy, of not being lovable, and so forth, and you can begin to release them. New feelings of being worthy of love take hold.

    Positive feelings are already present in everyone. There is a part of you that already knows that you are perfect as you are and that you are worthy of love. If your whole self agreed that you are imperfect and not worthy of love, there would be no inner conflict, and therefore no impetus in you to change that belief; it would be an open-and-shut case. You would deem your unworthiness an absolute truth and would have no motivation to change your thoughts and feelings. The purpose of spiritual work is not to impose something new and foreign on yourself; it is simply to acknowledge the truth you already know in some part of yourself and allow it to expand its influence. You might say that it is a seedling being choked by weeds; you are pulling out the weeds from around it so that it can grow into a beautiful plant.

A good way to reach nonjudgmental neutrality about yourself is to list facts about yourself. For example: "I sometimes interrupt people." "I'm very good at shopping." "I am angry at my mother." "I like watching reruns of *I Love Lucy*." "I wear size eight shoes." And so forth. Loving yourself does not imply that you ignore the facts about yourself. You simply do not make those facts wrong, although you may choose to change them if they can be changed. You certainly cannot change them if you do not know about them. In self-judgment, you try to change them because you think that you are a bad person and that you will become a good person if you change them. When you love yourself, you change them simply because doing so seems like the best choice.

You probably will not have much success changing your shoe size, but you can practice not interrupting others if you wish. You might find that not interrupting others makes your conversations more pleasant and helps you feel more peaceful. That is a good reason to change this habit.

However you feel is perfect as it is. You may feel happy, you may feel sad. You may feel sick, you may feel healthy. There is no right way to be a human being. By accepting the way something is for you at the moment, you are not necessarily putting much emphasis on it. If your body is sick, your acceptance of that fact does not glorify it—it is not making it more important than it is. It may be very important; it may not be. If you are neutral about it, you can see how important it really is and how much of your attention it requires. If you give unnecessary attention to a particular fact, you are taking energy away from other facts that might also benefit from your attention.

If you are not feeling very accepting, accept that you are

## ACCEPTANCE AND SOLVING PROBLEMS

not feeling accepting—you have to start where you are. If you are feeling unaccepting and then remember that you are "supposed" to be accepting, putting yourself down for not being accepting is missing the point. Whatever you experience is acceptable.

If you create karma by violating another person, you will pay the price for that. Of course, it is more pleasant if you do not create karma, but if you do, that, too, is acceptable—that is one way you learn on the physical plane. Virtually no one passes through the physical plane without creating and repaying karmas. Virtually no one passes through a single day without making mistakes, miscalculations, and so forth. Again, that is part of how you learn. That is acceptable. You are completely acceptable, exactly the way you are.

## 5 • BALANCE AND HEALING

Healing is a restoration to balance and wholeness. Everything you do to heal part of the whole affects the whole. Everything destructive to part of the whole is destructive to the whole. The whole does not stop at you personally. You have an influence on what is around you, both visible and invisible.

All healing has a spiritual or energetic aspect. Suppose, for instance, that you undertake to improve your nutrition. As you provide missing pieces to your body, it experiences more wholeness and, of course, you feel better. This positively affects your energetic atmosphere, as well as your intellect and emotions, because all levels of self work together. Likewise, if you clarify and strengthen your energy directly, your body will use the food it has more effectively.

Food itself, including vitamins and other supplements, has a spiritual component. Like people, some foods are "happier" than others. What makes people happy has many factors; the same is true of food. The soil on which it is raised will determine how whole it can become. If there are elements missing from the soil that, say, a carrot needs to be whole, it is less happy. If it is tended by gardeners who love the earth and respect its bounty, it is happier. It is the same as with human beings. People raised by parents who respect them and their place in the universe are usually happier—to begin with, at least—than those who are not.

Food is happier if it is fresh, transported carefully, stored properly, and prepared with a caring attitude. The last is the most important factor for those eating, because it is the food's most recent experience. Food also responds to your attitude as you consume it. If you create lovely surroundings in which to dine, perhaps with candles, a tablecloth, music, and so on, and pause to give thanks for your meal, your food tastes better. Not only is the food itself happier and more whole because of the energy given it, but you are in a more receptive state to receive what it has to give you.

Being eaten is food's fulfillment. It is the climax of a miraculous process of growth and transformation involving elements such as sunlight, water, soil, tiny seeds, and minerals that are invisible to you. It is all undertaken to present you with the gift of nourishment. Most people are thoughtless of this gift, and are often preoccupied when they eat. Perhaps they shovel their food down, in a hurry to get somewhere. Sometimes they read to give their minds something to do (perhaps so as not to taste the substandard food they are eating). Occasionally they fight with others. This is not a criticism—everyone has the right to choose his own relationship with food, just as with anything else in the universe. Nonetheless, people miss many of the simple joys of life because of lack of sensitivity and understanding. Eating is one instance of this loss.

The wholeness of food determines how much it has to give you physically, as well as mentally, emotionally, and spiritually. There is also the question of what foods to eat. Perhaps you have been consuming large amounts of canned spinach on Popeye's advice. Maybe you are cleaning your plate on a regular basis to help the children starving on other continents—you do not care too much what is on the plate, as long as it is clean when you are done. You may eat to fulfill certain cravings, not necessarily physical. Of course, there are more effective ways of choosing foods.

Your body needs certain elements. These needs change from day to day and even hour to hour. They relate to what you have eaten previously, your body's health, the type and amount of work you do, the climate and temperature, the time of year, and what is happening spiritually, mentally, and emotionally, both in you and in those around you, as well as many other factors. If your body's needs go unmet, it does its best to compensate. It calls substitutes to action, but this creates imbalance.

For example, if you do not eat enough protein, your body will begin to make use of the protein of your flesh itself. To rectify this imbalance, you would obviously eat more protein—not just any, but the type you need or can best assimilate. If a necessary vitamin is missing, your body tries to make do with another, perhaps using up the store of that one. This can create a domino effect. Your body starts being forced to act in a way it was not designed. If your body did not go into imbalance, it would simply die, so in a sense, this is beneficial. Still, your body is obviously not at its most efficient then.

Bookstores are overflowing with books expounding apparently contradictory theories about what you should eat. One theory states that you should eat a large variety of foods at one time. Another suggests that you should eat one food per meal. Some say that you should eat a vegetarian diet. Others claim that you will become malnourished if you do not eat meat. Finding the proper diet for yourself requires knowledge and intelligence, but you also will not find the diet that works for you if you do not learn to communicate with your body.

Actually, most people do communicate with their bodies, but it is often a one-way barrage of criticism. It is like a rider yelling at his horse and kicking it to go faster. Perhaps the horse has been trying to communicate for the last two miles that it has something stuck in its hoof, but the rider does not listen. Your body will tell you what it needs. To not only hear but understand, you must begin to listen and sense, putting aside your preconceptions and prejudices.

Sometimes people have cravings. These are not necessarily communications from the body as to what it truly needs. A craving for a candy bar may indicate that your body needs energy, but probably not that a Snickers bar is the optimal way to generate it. That is your interpretation. Messages from your body are usually subtler than cravings, but when you have a craving, if you listen, you may hear what the real message is.

When you are interested in eating, get quiet for a moment and ask your body if you actually want food now. If not, ask yourself why you are thinking about food. Perhaps an alarm clock went off in your mind: "It is 6:00—time to eat. I've eaten at 6:00 every night for the last forty years." Nevertheless, if your body does not want food and you do not need to eat at 6:00 for scheduling reasons, you might choose to wait. If your next opportunity to eat a meal is not until midnight, you might eat something light, or take a snack with you.

If the answer is yes, ask your body what it would like to eat. Do not jump to conclusions; take your time. If it is something you do not have and is not convenient for you to get at that moment, you might write it down on your shopping list. Also, you can ask your body what substitutes might be adequate for the time being. Maybe you do not have fresh shrimp, but canned salmon would be acceptable. While eating, continue to check in with your body periodically to see if you have had enough or if you would like something different.

Knowledge and intuition work together. Perhaps you have studied food combining. You had fruit salad and now your body is telling you that you would like eggs. Knowing that fruit is best eaten apart from heavy foods, you might wait until you digest it before eating eggs. You are acting on your intuition to eat eggs, and using your knowledge to guide how and when to eat them.

It is said that a little knowledge is dangerous. Applied insensitively, it can lead to more imbalance. For example, knowing that fruit is a cleanser, someone might eat only fruit. Cleansing can be valuable for the body, but it can be overdone. If an all-fruit diet is wrong for his body's metabolism, the time of year, the quality of the fruit available, or whatever, he will increase his body's imbalance. If he is simply carrying out a predetermined program based on a little knowledge, he is not listening to his body. If he were listening, he would know that diet is not working for him.

It may be wise to experiment with different diets. Try one approach for a while and see how it feels; then try another. You can learn much from this. If something is supposed to be "good" but does not make you feel more balanced, it is not right for you. Suppose that you feel that your body is telling you to eat watermelon, and you do. If you feel refreshed and balanced afterwards, acknowledge that you accurately understood your body. Noticing what that felt like will help you develop discernment.

You cannot heal yourself fully just through eating balancing food. Nonetheless, this is an area where you can practice skills that will lead to finding balance in other aspects of your life. We used food as an example because it is something you deal with virtually every day. Our purpose here is not to discuss food per se, but healing—making whole. You can apply these points to other areas of your life, staying alert to the spiritual aspect in all things. By working with it intelligently and creatively, you can promote wholeness.

Perhaps you are hearing from within that you need to spend some time in the country. It could be your body telling you that the city's pollution is beginning to take its toll. It may be your mind saying that it needs some rest or a change. It may be your emotions longing for communion with plants and the earth itself. Perhaps your essence is nudging you to go to a particular place so you can meet someone who will bring something valuable into your life.

If you are simply being drawn to any beautiful, quiet, natural spot for a few days, you have a wide range of choices. If there is someone to meet, obviously you need to choose the right one. Perhaps you keep thinking of a particular place. That is probably the place that would be best. Beware of talking yourself out of it, thinking it is too expensive, crowded, or "I didn't like it the last time I went."

We are not suggesting that you blindly follow such impulses, but you owe it to yourself to check them out further. You could make some phone calls to see if it really is too expensive. You might remember someone you know there with whom you could stay. If you move even a little with your inner direction, doors tend to open before you.

Your whole being seeks balance and wholeness, seeks to fill in what is missing and correct what is out of proportion. Conscious cooperation with the process is like skillfully piloting a ship that is already moving toward its destination.

What is missing most for the majority of people is a full and healthy spirituality. This is true even for many who are deeply religious. This lack causes the greatest amount of compensation of any lack in human life. Spiritual malnutrition is eventually more debilitating than physical hunger. Spiritual lack is not fulfilled in the same way as physical lack. Physical hunger can be completely satisfied from external food. Spiritual hunger ultimately must be satisfied from within. A person can eat the most delicious and nutritious spiritual food and not assimilate it because of a lack of openness; therefore, she is not nourished. Still, opening to spiritual food from outside yourself *can* help you open to it from within.

Everyone came into the physical plane willing to be imbalanced for a while. You knew that this was part of the package. The act of finding balance teaches many lessons and leads to much growth. It is not wrong to be imbalanced. We do encourage our students, though, not to maintain imbalance longer than necessary.

In a way, the creation of imbalance signals the start of the game. Rather than sitting there decrying the imbalance, perhaps feeling sorry for yourself, waiting around for someone to come fix it, be aware that the bell has rung—the game has begun. The rebalancing results in much satisfaction—that is winning the game. Then, you probably will decide to start a new one.

    The game is not that difficult or painful if you really play it. If you do not know how to play it, you can learn. In any case, everyone will win the game. There is no question about that. Everyone will find balance. All you experience conspires to push you toward balance. To change analogies, each time you slam into a wall, you have the opportunity to learn to move instead toward the open door. Some people move right to the door without slamming into walls, or even stubbing their toes much. Others make quite a number of indentations in their walls.

    Our purpose as teachers is to help people move toward the open doors and avoid slamming into walls when possible. There will be at least a few walls for everyone. Those who have slammed into many walls are going to become quite expert in helping others avoid walls in the future. No experience is ultimately lost or wasted. Still, the game is more fun when you play it more consciously and go directly to the open doors.

*If everything is seeking balance, why are we so easily triggered into imbalance?*

When you binge on food that you crave but that is disruptive to you, or when your temper flares and you get into an old pattern with someone, you are actually moving toward balance. The reason is that imbalanced elements latent in you are being activated and brought to the surface, where you can deal with and release them. The imbalance was there all along. The point is not to avoid being triggered at all costs, in the name of maintaining balance, but to use triggering as a tool for growth.

*Are people meant to eat meat?*

We cannot make a general statement on this. Some bodies are better suited to meat-eating than others. In our view, eating meat is not a black-or-white issue. It is conceivable that everyone could successfully be a vegetarian if all the other necessary elements were present—a big "if." On the other hand, meat consumption is not a violation of the human body per se. There are people who find even red meat to be beneficial, at least at certain times. Generally, the greater the stress in their lives, the more that meat can be helpful, especially if they are used to it. For one thing, it can help them feel more grounded. Some people also have a greater need for high-quality protein than others, and meat is an acceptable way to obtain it. However, many people in affluent cultures eat more, often much more, than they need to satisfy their protein requirements, and this can be destructive.

The conditions under which animals are raised and killed, and meat is stored, prepared, served, and eaten all affect the energy of meat, and how beneficial it is to your body. The most important single factor is how animals are killed. If there is much pain, that is reflected in the meat. Eating meat itself is not immoral, in our opinion, but causing unnecessary pain and suffering to animals is.

## MEDITATION

Imagine a great force coming into your body bringing healing power. Feel everything in your body being in exquisite and perfect balance. Do the same with your mind, emotions, and spirit.

# Part II

# THE NATURE OF ENERGY

## 6 • RELEASING BLOCKS

All energy comes from and returns to the Tao. Energy is like a river that forms at a great sea and passes through a beautiful terrain of mountains, valleys, and other landscapes. Sometimes it breaks up into several branches and then recombines, until it eventually reunites with the sea.

The river of energy flowing to and from the Tao enjoys the whole trip, you might say; it is not impatient about returning, yet it is its nature to move. It is not moving merely to return to the great sea; it is moving because it must.

All things seek unity. Bringing peace is not primarily a matter of convincing people to try to get along, but of removing blocks to the natural movement toward unity. There is a growing impetus toward unity now. The blocks that resist it feel increased pressure.

The natural state is one in which there is free movement of energy. Maturity is the ability to let energy move freely at a high level. It is a learned skill, one of the main skills you are learning on the physical plane. Every life experience teaches you something about letting energy move more freely and/or on a higher level. You may not interpret it that way, but you could.

The more freely your energy moves, the more joy you experience. Think of the joy in a young child. She does not yet have a mature capacity to let energy move, but she has few blocks, so she enjoys the energy she has. That is why children are often such a pleasure to be around. To recapture this feeling, it is not necessary to go back to childhood. The key is actually to go forward, releasing your adult blocks. If you do this, your joy will be far greater than what children experience because your capacity is greater. You may not be able to release all your blocks in this lifetime, but it is a worthy goal to work toward.

A block is like a piece of fruit: it comes off the tree easily when it is ripe. When it is not, you can pull hard on it and it still might not come off. Also, fruit might not ripen at all if the tree is not nurtured.

When you identify a block, you are really identifying a lesson. Lessons last as long as they need to. An aspect of self may be like a tree that needs much water, sunshine, fertilizer, and pruning before its fruit is ready to fall into your hand, but the fruit may be extraordinary when it does. It may enrich your life more from its lessons than another fruit that took less time to ripen.

Work on your blocks, but do not try to force them to release. Love the parts of yourself that need greater understanding and allow them to reveal themselves to you a step at a time.

It is not necessary to work on releasing blocks all the time; sometimes you need to go out and play. On the other hand, spending a little time with them on a continual basis can yield much benefit. Trying to do it all at once, or working on them sporadically, such as when you attend workshops, is less effective than constant care, even if it is only ten minutes a day.

## 7 • MOVEMENT

Energy is universal material that is charged, which causes it to move. The Tao is not energy; it has no charge—it simply is. From what is, energy emanates. The more you simply are, the more energy emanates from you. It emanates from a place that is not energy. To make an analogy, an electrical plant makes energy; the plant itself is not electricity.

Because energy is charged and moves substance (which is energy vibrating more slowly), it can heal. In most disease, there is a state of nonmovement. Energy stimulates movement in what is stuck if it is willing and ready to move. A person who has no blocks could theoretically handle an infinite amount of energy. In application, this is not practical because of the density of the human body. There are resistances built into it that are natural and necessary for its existence. Most people, however, are underenergized, and this is the source of many difficulties.

To be able to withstand high intensities of healing energy, the physical body must be strong. It was, for example, useful to Jesus that he walked so much; it made his body stronger and better able to withstand the intensity coming through it. Exercise itself is, of course, healing to the body. People who exercise a lot are often able to "get away with" more abuse to their body. Exercise keeps toxins moving out, as does flushing the body with pure water, another example of movement bringing healing. Too much water or exercise can be detrimental, so there is a balance.

Every healing technique promotes movement in one way or another. The art of healing is knowing what needs to move. Sound waves are a form of energy in motion. Proper sounds can move blocks. Light is also energy in motion; many people meditate on light for this reason.

Movement is needed on all levels of self. The word "emotion" is mostly the word "motion." Expressing emotions appropriately allows them to move, promoting emotional healing. Thoughts also need to move. A thought going round and round in your head is like a bird that keeps flying into a window. If you express and clarify it, perhaps by writing it down and working with it, it is like opening a window.

Children can benefit from being taught to move on all levels. They can make healing sounds, such as through chant, and can learn to move in beautiful ways that allow their bodies' energies to be free. Children should not be forced into movement patterns that are contrary to the ways their bodies want to move. For example, those who are not suited to ballet will not benefit from lessons in it, and may even be harmed by them. Those who are suited to it will likely enjoy them. Singing for children is important in moving their energy. Children who sing a lot are likely to be healthier than those who do not. They should be encouraged to make up songs. Adults can also benefit from doing this.

Love is the highest form of energy; therefore, love is the greatest healer. Every other form of healing is a manifestation of love. Loving is the most significant contribution you can make to the well-being of others. Most people have a quite limited experience of love. No matter how much love you have, you can always experience more. You are on earth to increase your experience of love, and to increase love itself. In fact, increasing love is the purpose of all existence.

## 8 • BEING CONSTRUCTIVE

A constructive intent is based in love. It is the intent to bless, to foster the well-being of all. A destructive intent is based in fear. It is malevolence, the intent to harm. A destructive intent carries within itself the seeds of its own destruction, since that is its nature. To fulfill itself, it must destroy itself.

Most people have a combination of constructive and destructive intents. The goal of the spiritual path is to be solely constructive. This does not happen just because you make a conscious decision to be constructive "from now on." A conscious decision certainly can begin the process, but you must deal with your destructive intents and develop the ability to function fully constructively. The desire to live fully from a constructive intent is not the same as actually being able to do it.

It is like waking up one day and saying, "I wish to be in top physical condition." This does not mean that because you made this decision, you will materialize it. It does not matter how much you visualize yourself in top condition, affirm that you are in it, and want it. Those are excellent starting points, but the decision has to be carried out by your whole being. You need to start doing what will move you toward top physical condition and dealing with the blocks that come up. You might say, "I'm going to exercise six hours a day," but that could put you in worse physical condition. To achieve top physical condition, you would need to develop sensitivity to your body's needs. That includes discerning what types of exercises are best, when to do them, and in what combinations; what foods are appropriate at what times; what certain signals mean; and so forth. In other words, top physical condition must be developed from the inside out. You cannot arbitrarily impose it on yourself.

Similarly, to become fully constructive one must go

through a process from within. If you make an intellectual decision and try to impose being fully constructive on yourself from the outside, you are likely to make mistakes similar to those of a person who decides to exercise six hours a day. You may lack sensitivity to your true needs. You may try to live according to dogma or programming that being constructive requires you to behave in certain ways, such as smiling all the time or always being "nice." It is better to see yourself as moving in the direction of total constructiveness rather than pretending to already be there, letting it emerge naturally as you learn what really is constructive.

Here is another analogy: you wish to fly your plane to Brussels. As you move in that direction, you keep going off course and must make constant adjustments. You overshoot in one direction and then the other. As you get closer and closer, you veer off the trajectory less and less; your errors are almost imperceptible. In real life, you usually do not reach Brussels, or total constructiveness, but you can get close to it. If you allow yourself to be a person who is in movement toward this goal, rather than trying to be someone who is already there, you will be truly constructive more often. It is not a significant problem that you veer off course now and then as long as you correct it and keep moving.

*In Hinduism, the great triad of gods is Brahma, Shiva, and Vishnu—the creator, destroyer, and preserver. How would you relate that to what you're saying?*

These "gods" correlate with the affirming (positive), denying (negative), and stabilizing (neutral) forces. They are all used to achieve intent, whatever it is. They are necessary and must be in balance.

The denying force says no. It cleanses, eliminates, and breaks things down, like a leaf in a compost pile. Breaking down compost makes new growth possible. Growth is achieved by the affirming force. It says yes. It builds and moves forward. The stabilizing force is neutral and provides a bridge. Trees grow in the spring and summer (affirming), lose their leaves in the autumn (denying), and rest in the winter (stabilizing). All stages are part of the creative cycle.

The denying force is necessary for movement and growth. If you were to drive a car on a road without resistance, both from the roughness of the road and the tread on the tires, you would slide off the road, or you simply would not move. The friction thrusts you forward. When you decide to do something major in your life, there are likely to be roadblocks both in yourself and externally. In dealing with these roadblocks, you propel yourself forward. As you reach your destination, the roadblocks dissolve, and you find neutrality. Then you begin again.

The denying force is like darkness. If all were light, nothing could exist. Light and darkness must interact. Darkness here refers to what is unformed, like the night sky between the stars and other celestial bodies. The denying force is resistant or inert, but it is not necessarily destructive.

If you are motivated by love, you wish to be constructive, to benefit rather than hinder yourself and others. You can direct your affirming, denying, and stabilizing forces in such a way that the most constructive results occur. There are times when you use a denying force for a constructive purpose, such as saying no forcefully when that will bring the highest outcome. There are also times when an affirming force is used for a destructive purpose, such as allowing something that hurts others.

As you move toward total constructiveness, you are moving toward total love, or *agape*.

# 9 • WORKING WITH ENERGY

## THE FUNDAMENTAL ELEMENT

Although people do not normally deal with energy directly, it is the most fundamental element of human life. Energy emanates from the consciousness of its source; your overall energy emanates from your overall consciousness. If your energy does not feel good, there is something in your consciousness that needs attention. There is no reason your energy cannot feel good most of the time.

It is difficult to maintain a healthy attitude when your atmosphere is dense and heavy. It is vital to keep energy pouring through it to clean it.

## NEGATIVE ENERGY

*Sometimes people say that there's negative energy in a particular place. I feel that energy is energy, and it's the way you perceive it that makes it negative or positive.*

We do not entirely agree. Some energies are beneficent, healing, and pleasant to be in; others are unpleasant. For example, if you walk into a room after there has been a vicious argument, it does not feel good to be there. You may know nothing about the argument, but you can feel it if you have some sensitivity. That would be an example of negative energy.

*So, you are saying that there are two kinds of energy in the entire realm of reality?*

There are infinite kinds of energy. Every person, animal, plant, mineral—in fact every consciousness—has a unique energy, but energies are based on either love or fear, or a mixture. Energies based on love feel good. Energies based on fear do not. Energies based on a fairly equal and blended mixture of both love and fear feel more or less neutral. The intent behind an energy determines its basis. The intent to be beneficial gives an energy a basis in love. The intent to be detrimental gives an energy a basis in fear.

There are three kinds of forces: creative, destructive, and neutral. There is nothing wrong with the destructive force. It is at work, for instance, when you burn logs for necessary heat and light. In the case of the vicious argument, however, the destructive force is used with the intent to cause detriment. The resulting energy, being fear-based, does not feel good.

## THE MOST DIRECT ROUTE

Energy moves in the most direct possible route. If there is more than one direct route available and enough energy, the energy will use all of them.

## HELPING

Healing energy brings up what needs to be healed, and it is not always comfortable. If you are empathetic, you feel others' discomfort in their healing process. You may interpret it as your own discomfort; it is not always easy to stay objective enough to see what is actually going on. If you experience a change in the way you feel when you are around another person, you can usually assume that what you are feeling is not originating in you (provided he is not triggering a reaction in you). Consider it information. It can help you decide how to interact with him.

There is a balance to be maintained. If you are too sympathetic, you tend to take on the other person's energies. If you are not empathetic, you will not be of any aid. You may choose to withdraw because it is not appropriate for you to do something, or because you do not feel capable of doing something—perhaps you have your own needs to meet. Or of course, you may wish to offer help.

## WORKSHOPS

*I was at a workshop where the participants were experiencing a lot of pain. I didn't know how to protect myself. We had an anger exercise—many had been abused children—and people were screaming and hollering. I let the energy go through me. It completely tired me.*

At least you knew enough to let it keep moving through you. That is important. As long as it did not stay in you, it did no long-term harm. You were helping others process. That was a valuable service. If a large part of a group is processing, particularly if they are not accustomed to it, there need to be several people not processing, preferably on staff, supporting them. Your workshop may have been understaffed. It should not have been exhausting for the participants not processing. Without adequate staff, such workshops can be draining for everyone.

## ENERGY AS LOVE

Normally, love is thought of as an emotional experience, bringing smiles or perhaps tears. Love, however, can manifest on every level. When love manifests in the body as pure healing energy, it brings peace and alignment to it.

## 10 • ECSTASY

When we speak through this channel, we usually spend several minutes in preparation first. We silently work with the energy of the person or people present to purify it of what might be called psychic debris. We then raise it to a higher vibration, so that healing on all levels can take place. Words often distract somewhat from energetic receptivity, although they can generate insights that lead to increased energy, so we do not discourage words. Receiving insight is similar to receiving energy. You might say that insight is intellectual healing energy, and loving inspiration is emotional healing energy. Each is needed, in addition to pure, kinetic energy; one does not live by pure energy alone.

There are higher and lower levels of intellectual, emotional, and kinetic energies. Higher energies are not better than lower energies. Higher energies are broad and encompassing, while lower energies are specific and focused. Higher energies vibrate at a faster rate, making them more intense and catalytic.

On the physical plane, higher kinetic energy is more accessible than higher emotional and intellectual energies. The latter usually only come forth in periods of pressure. For example, if a person having a crisis turns to God, whatever that means to him, he may have a transcendent experience of inspiration, an opening to greater love and empathy. Another example is someone working intensely on a problem. If he lets go of it for a moment, he might experience a "lightning bolt" of penetrating insight in which much understanding falls into place.

If you are open enough to them, inspiration and insight you receive externally can trigger higher energy experiences. In addition, being surrounded and permeated by higher pure kinetic energy from an external source, such as ourselves, can give you a sense of what it feels like. If you open to it and resonate with it, it can help you access it from within.

In a higher energetic state, your body feels transcendent, even ecstatic, similar to "getting high." Although most people who have the experience enjoy it, they do not really want it to last too long. Ecstasy is an unknown experience, and tends to generate fear. The more you practice it, though, the longer you can sustain it.

Another way to open to higher kinetic energy experiences is through physical stresses such as athletic challenges. The stresses can force a letting go. A similar but more gentle way is through dance: the rhythm of music allied with movement can bring a dancer into a trance state, in which he is lifted into selfless awareness, and the beauty of his art can take wing.

The goal of your essence is ecstasy. Most people settle for coping. In a sense, the early part of life is preparation for ecstasy. You often get karmic repayments out of the way, usually by your early thirties. In your middle thirties, you emphasize shedding your imprinting (social conditioning). In your late thirties or your forties, you might begin to do your major life work, which is when ecstasy is the most available, although it can be experienced any time. Infants have some experience of ecstasy when their situations are not stressful. Ecstasy can be reached in meditation. The key is letting go, not just letting go of this thing or that but a total letting go.

It is not intended that intense ecstasy be a continual experience. When you get used to it, it is not ecstasy anymore but your norm. Ecstasy then ascends to a new level. Everyday experience for one person might be ecstasy for another, if he could somehow open to that level. It is the influx of something higher or greater that gives the "rush" known as ecstasy. Evolution could be defined as the expansion that allows this to occur, either quickly or slowly.

# ECSTASY

It is not possible to constantly make large jumps in what you can accommodate of higher experience. You move to a higher level and then need to assimilate the changes, integrate that new experience so that it becomes the foundation for the next expansion. Ecstasy, however, can be a greater part of life than people usually think.

Since you are at different levels in the many aspects of your life, there are varying levels of ecstasy possible. You may be functioning at a lower level in your career, for instance, than in the artwork you do as a hobby. The amount of ecstasy you experience depends on how big a jump from your previous experience it represents.

Relationships are a key aspect of life. Suppose that you and your partner have a breakthrough: you make a deeper contact with each other, essence to essence. This would bring a feeling of ecstasy. The amount of rush would be commensurate with the amount of additional depth you achieved compared to what you had previously shared. The quality of the energy would reflect the level of the relationship.

Many little steps are as valuable as one big one. The greatest rushes tend to come after releasing large resistances that were previously preventing expansion. Without substantial resistance, growth tends to be more gradual, although there are still natural variations in its rate, just as there are variations in the rate at which children grow physically.

Higher emotional energies can usually be most easily experienced through music, because music can bypass emotional blocks more easily than other forms of inspiration. Intellectual ecstasy is most easily known through philosophy in which the amazing perfection of life, the awesome order of all evolution, is glimpsed. You could experience this when a simple truth about everyday life penetrates and opens you to a transcendent understanding, but most people are not fluid enough in their understanding to permit this. The same is true of higher emotional experiences: another person's pure, loving act or word could inspire at least a small opening, allowing for an experience of higher emotional energy, but again, this is rarely permitted.

The source of ecstasy is essence contact. Your essence is your higher self, your link to the rest of the universe. Expansion allows you to experience more of it—that is why it feels so good. When you contact another person's essence, basically the same thing happens, only there is a multiplication because two essences are involved.

The spiritual path is not one of accumulating information or theories; it is a path of opening and developing your facility to receive more and more, to see farther and farther, and to be capable of handling with grace higher and higher challenges. All this leads to a state of *agape*, which is the ultimate transcendent experience. *Agape* is enlightenment.

We are all part of infinity. There is no end to the expansion that can occur for us. However, the physical plane is more susceptible than any other to the influences of limitation. It is easy to get stuck. People can live their entire lives trapped in harsh and narrow belief structures. Experiencing ecstasy is much more difficult on the physical plane than on others. Therefore, any relatively small opening to ecstasy is a major occurrence, and one for which you can rightfully congratulate yourself.

If you notice the beauty of a flower as you are walking, and stop to truly see and make contact with it for a moment, you will have done more than most of those who are exposed to flowers. Even those who love to garden and feel some sort of a kinship with flowers rarely stop to actually make a direct, real-time contact with them.

The greatest ecstasy available is that which blends all the higher energies. This is extremely rare on the physical plane, but is sometimes experienced in sex. When you are having sex with someone you truly love, and you make a genuine contact with him or her, you can have a higher emotional experience; it can be quite inspiring. As your bodies deeply let go, you can have a higher kinetic experience. If, in the midst of this, you are intellectually present, clear, and open, you can glimpse the cosmic order, bringing a higher intellectual experience. If these three experiences occur simultaneously, it is the highest experience available to human beings. Such intensity and true intimacy is frightening for most people. It leaves you highly vulnerable, yet paradoxically, very strong.

All the work you do to release fear and to heal your psyche is good work, leading toward the possibility of such openness. Most people never have such a transcendent experience, yet their lives are not wasted. Every experience everyone has ever had can contribute in one way or another toward evolution. Sometimes experiences only point more clearly to what not to do next time. That is a necessary part of growth. Still, it is beneficial to be aware of what is possible. It is like a carrot dangling in front of you. It reminds you that all the work you have done and are doing is worth the effort: ecstasy is possible.

Physical-plane life is often difficult, but it is ultimately what you make it. Through all the difficulties, you can learn to experience joy on a continual basis. Your well for holding joy grows larger and deeper as you move along through your little and large experiences of ecstasy.

When growth is blocked, you feel frustration and anxiety, but once larger blocks do move, larger ecstasies can result. It does not really matter whether your growth consists of serial doses of ecstasy in smaller quantities, or sporadic but larger bursts of ecstasy, although steadier growth is less stressful. The point is that you continue to grow. As long as you do, you have fulfillment and carry the sense that your life is worthwhile.

# Part III

# HEALING PRACTICE

# 11 • HEALING OTHERS

## OFFERING

Your presence itself offers healing. The more conscious you are of your powerful healing presence, the more directly you can bring it to bear. You do not really need confidence that you can do it. You simply need to do it. You gain confidence by experiencing yourself doing it. The more experience you have of yourself as a healer, as a being of healing power, the less you feel that you need to rely on external sources as the primary factor in healing.

Thought is powerful. When your thoughts become clearer, you offer greater clarity to others.

Although you can offer a great deal, you ultimately cannot heal another. Each person must accept healing.

## FREEDOM FROM LIMITATION

The more that those around someone ill are free of limitations in consciousness about him, the easier it is for him to throw off limitations himself. For instance, you do not have to believe that he is not going to die, but it is vital that you not believe that he will. You can be neutral on the subject, rather than imposing a limitation on the circumstance. If he believes that he is dying, we suggest that you neither agree nor disagree.

Likewise, you do not need to believe that he is going to experience a miraculous healing, but neither should you believe that he cannot. There is nothing impossible. What good is a negative belief to you or to anyone? Virtually no human being has completely let go of limitations, but it is important that there be no unnecessary limitations around someone ill. One reason for working with affirmations and visualizations is that there are fewer limitations in the imagination. Imagining recovery, for instance, when it looks unlikely, can help erase unnecessary limitations.

## HEALING ENVIRONMENT

Your consciousness is always filled with something. If it is filled with beauty, humor, inspiration, and so forth, it supports healing. If someone ill does not have a lot of ability to keep his consciousness focused, those around him can help him by creating a healing environment, with plants, music, art, inspirational recordings, and so on.

## INTUITION

*Where does one draw the line with intuition? I really don't know what I'm doing in terms of healing, but I have a strong feeling to get up and touch _____ (a woman I know in the row in front of me).*

If you feel guided to touch someone with a loving intent in an appropriate situation, it probably would do no harm, so you have nothing to lose by going with your intuition in that regard. On the other hand, if you are getting an impulse to perform brain surgery and you are not a surgeon, we would suggest that you wait. If you are in doubt, ask the other person.

## INTENT

If you wish to have a healing influence, clear yourself and put distracting thoughts aside. Relax, and have the intent that healing move from you to the other person. Healing can occur through something as simple as touching someone with a loving intent. Children, especially infants, can experience remarkable healing in this way. Intent is more important than technique. However, if you have both intent and technique, your effectiveness increases.

## ABILITY TO HEAL OTHERS

Native ability in healing is like native ability in music. You may be quite musical, but if you do not have a technical background in music, know any instruments or even any songs, it may be appropriate to get some training if you wish to express yourself musically. There are an abundance of classes and books on healing that can be helpful. A knowledge of basic anatomy and physiology can be useful; learning what the different body parts do is available to anyone. The best way to learn to heal, though, is to work with a good healer.

## HEALING RITUAL

Energy work can be quite effective long-distance, but doing it in person has a symbolic advantage. The person receiving the energy sees your belief that she can heal. The ritual is an instruction to heal, so to speak. Still, the energy itself is primary.

## APPROACHES TO HEALING

There are two basic approaches to healing another person energetically, both of them valid. In one, you work more in your own body. You bring his energy pattern into it, cleanse and change it, and give it back, so to speak. In the other, you work primarily in his body. You stimulate his own healing energy to come forth and move the illness out. You can also use a combination of these methods. Both can use a lot of your energy and be draining, although the second one is generally less so and is better if you are not physically very strong. If you are actually weak, you should not be doing this work.

    A variation on the second approach is to just offer

loving support. You surround the person with energy, letting him receive what he can, without attempting to go into his body and change his pattern too much. This is useful when a person is fragile and a major change might be too much of a shock. The priority is helping him become stronger, so he can withstand and adapt to a change in his energetic pattern.

If someone's pattern is very distorted, you are better off not bringing it into your body unless you are sure that you can handle it. The same is true for someone quite weak; he may drain you too much. On the other hand, if his own healing core is not very accessible, you might want to bring his pattern into your body as a kind of jump-start.

Otherwise, the approach you use depends on your preference and intuition about the specific situation.

## HEALING IS RECIPROCAL

Working with a loved one who is ill is a process of healing not just for him but for everyone concerned—everyone's issues arise. It is a group process focused in the person who is ill. Your work supports not just his healing but that of everyone else, and their healing supports yours. Meeting your issues encourages the others to meet theirs and increases the healing momentum of the group process. Resisting your issues reduces it. All the players in a healing event play off one another, although that is not often recognized. So when you seek to offer healing to another, do not neglect your own healing.

## 12 • THE MEDICAL ESTABLISHMENT

Orthodox medical science has virtually no conscious experience with higher energy. When medical doctors come across patients for whom orthodox medicine held no hope and who are healed by higher energy (or by holistic techniques), they often do not know what to make of it, and therefore do not make anything of it. It is simply not in their paradigm.

Someone incapable of learning the lessons of his illness, making changes, and receiving healing energy may be wise to entrust himself completely to his doctors, having nothing else to which to entrust himself. If you *are* capable of those things, though, it is wise to commit completely to that route. You can still receive medical care, seeing it as supporting your healing rather than as your main vehicle for healing. In fact, you can see everything you do as supporting your healing. In some cases, medical treatment can be very useful. At least, it may be useful to control symptoms and pain while you open further to your own healing power and give your body what it needs.

Doctors are a healing force for others most when they offer healing energy. Many do this unconsciously and a few are conscious of it. There are doctors who are great healers—whatever they do usually works to some extent, no matter what it is. Their patients believe in them and therefore believe that the medicine the doctors give them will help—their belief helps make it so. Doctors often make much of the placebo effect with natural remedies, but it is just as much a factor with establishment medicine. Strong belief encourages you to open to your healing energy, allowing the best possible results. So much the better if the medicine actually provides the body with something it needs.

Hospitals should be places of healing energy. They are usually the opposite of that—places where the focus is on the absence of healing rather than on the source of healing. Unless someone in that environment knows how to put a protective "bubble" around himself, whatever healing energy he opens to tends to be drawn away. He is in a vacuum because there is so little healing energy around him. It is like heat rushing out of a building on a cold day when a door is opened.

    It would be a wonderful thing if everyone working in hospitals were trained to open to their healing energy. People who are new to their profession come in fairly open, but shut down over time because the demand on them is so great; they feel they have to protect themselves, and they do, although shutting down is not the optimal way of doing it.

# 13 • HOW BLOCKED EMOTIONS FEEL

When you are doing healing work, it is useful to know what various blocked or stuck emotions can feel like energetically. This helps you identify them and assist in their release. It takes practice to learn how to discern energies. You might feel nothing at first, but if you keep listening, you will develop your discernment.

These perceptions are somewhat subjective, but here are some guidelines on how blocked emotions feel energetically:

Anger, conscious or unconscious, feels like uncomfortably hot energy that wants to move out but is being held back.

Rage is anger exaggerated. It feels hotter and more pressurized, like the sensation of almost scalding yourself with steam.

Anxiety feels like anger or even rage anesthetized, insulated in thick shock-absorbing pads wrapped too tightly. It's emotional.

Worry feels like a constricted cesspool of fear sloshing around. It's intellectual.

Fear feels cold or cool. It is energy withdrawing, contracted, creating a vacuum, an emptiness, but not a calm, peaceful void. It is imbalanced.

If the fear is old, defenses have likely been generated. Brittleness usually indicates fear, and over time, a thick wall or armor can develop, in which case the fear may not be obvious—it is within the armor. You will probably not feel it until the armor dissolves.

Panic is fear energy that cannot withdraw. It is chaotic, fast and irregular in its movements. It does not have time to become frozen stiff or to build a wall. Quivering indicates something between fear and panic. Terror is fear exaggerated.

## OPENING TO HEALING

Stubbornness is a form of fear. You might feel it as a cold, long vertical stiffness.

Fear and anger go hand in hand. Sometimes fear comes first, sometimes anger. Where there is fear, as it subsides there tends to be anger—anger at what was feared. When fear is great, anger goes underground, so do not be surprised if you find anger after rooting out fear; that is part of the healing of the fear. Likewise, where there is anger, there is often unacknowledged fear below that. So after anger is released, you might sense the fear that caused the angry reaction. You generally do not repress anger at people unless you also fear the possible consequences of expressing it. Fear and anger are two sides of a polarity; fear is the feminine pole and anger is the masculine. Everything that feels unpleasant is a form of fear and anger. Everything that feels good is a form of love.

## 14 • ENERGIES IN THE BODY

Every part of the body represents or mirrors a part of the psyche. When you are doing healing work, it is significant where in the body you find a particular symptom or energy. Looking at what the part does for the body helps you see more readily what it symbolizes. The ankle helps the body move forward. With a tight ankle, there is difficulty doing so, possibly in more ways than just physical—it may express that the person does not want to. A sprained or broken ankle, more so.

However, as with the psyche, the body's dynamics cannot be defined too narrowly or interpreted too rigidly; a specific symptom or energy can mean many different things. If you have several ideas of what body parts, symptoms, and energies can represent, you are more likely to sense what is actually occurring, rather than imposing a predetermined view on your perceptions. Also, there's always the possibility that a symptom is mostly or entirely physical.

If, for example, you pick up tightness in someone's calf, it could simply be soreness from a physical strain. It is also possible that he has sadness that makes it tighter than it would normally be, contributing to his straining it. There are several other possible factors.

Still, we will make some generalizations based on our observations about what issues tend to show up in particular parts of the body. This is not meant to be a comprehensive list, and does not necessarily contradict what has been written elsewhere when it differs. It is meant to give you some additional possibilities to consider:

Jaw: Self-control, tension.
Shoulders: Responsibility, guilt, the need to protect oneself, feeling burdened.
Upper spine: Loss.
Middle spine: Guilt, feelings related to sexual drive,

issues about the ability to have what one wants sexually. Heat in this area may indicate sexual frustration. Heat in the groin may indicate conflict with a partner or anger about sex.

Lower spine: Finances.

Whole spine: Practical intelligence, street smarts. The spine carries out the intelligence of the brain. If the spine is burning, the person may not feel capable of applying intelligence to daily life. This is often someone excessively theoretical. You may want to check out the brain for tension.

Whole back: Belief systems. Everyone has belief systems. If the belief system is comfortable in the life, the back is at ease. If the belief system cannot handle what comes, the back is tight or nervous.

When people hold hands, it indicates a heart connection. The hands can be an extension of the heart. Both hands and eyes need to be balanced in giving and receiving. If more energy comes in than goes out, or vice versa, eventually there will be a problem. This only happens if there is a block where energy gathers, trying to get through. If the block does not release, symptoms ensue. In a healthy person, energy is moving in and out continually, although there is more inflow during sleep and more outflow during waking hours. During times of healing, there is also more inflow than outflow, but this does not necessarily create an imbalance, because the energy is being used to fill a need; it is not stuck.

The female breasts provide milk, and by extension, nurturing and nourishment. It is no accident that it is near the heart. The heart is the neutral space in which the Tao can come forth. It can also provide the connection between the emotions and the intellect. Emotions are mostly seated below the heart, in the "guts," and the intellect is mostly above the heart, in the head.

When the heart is "broken" through great

disappointment, the grief is held close to the heart when it is fresh. In time, it is pushed farther away from the heart. It becomes heaviness or armor in the chest, or a burden in the shoulders.

The chest relates to vulnerability. If someone is proud of himself, he sticks his chest out—he feels that he can withstand scrutiny. Someone whose chest is caved in fears that others will be hard on him. If the chest feels weak, there is a self-worth issue and vulnerability to being demeaned by others—not just criticism of some act, but a demeaning of the self.

Buttocks: Shame, which might be fixated on sex and bodily functions, but it is from the standpoint that one does not have the right to be here.

Legs can tell you a variety of things. If they feel leaden, it generally indicates that the body seems heavy, and the legs cannot support it without likewise being heavy. It also suggests that life in general feels too hard. This is not the same as the burdens carried in the shoulders, which are more an issue of the complications of life, other people and situations to handle. The shoulders are closer to the brain, and its issues are more intellectual.

If, on the other hand, the legs feel overly light and lacking in substance, it might indicate that the person is not adequately in his body.

The upper legs can relate to sex or childbearing. Ambivalence about these things can manifest as pain, tightness, and/or a lack of flexibility in movement. If the upper legs feel rubbery, either in the hips or the knees, there is often an unwillingness to take responsibility for sexual or childbearing issues.

The calves often carry sadness about other people and their acts. For example, you might store feelings here about how your parents treated your brothers and sisters, whereas sadness about how they treated you would likely be in your chest.

The feet have to do with groundedness—how connected you are to the earth.

# 15 • CHAKRAS

Chakras, your energy centers, are well covered in other texts, but here are a few additional comments: To review, the first or root chakra is at the top of your pelvic bone (from the back it is at the base of your spine). The second or spleen chakra is about the width of two fingers below your navel. The third or solar plexus chakra is in your diaphragm cavity, usually about three inches above your navel. The fourth or heart chakra is in the center of your breastbone. The fifth or throat chakra is at the base of your neck. The sixth or third eye chakra is just above the center of your eyebrows. The seventh or crown chakra is at the top of your head, about two-thirds back. The eighth, ninth, and higher chakras are above your head in your spiritual body. There are other chakras in the body, in the hands and feet, for instance, that are not numbered. Exact locations of the chakras vary from individual to individual depending partly on the size and proportions of the body.

The heart chakra is the center of the chakras, providing connection, mediation, and consolidation between what is above and what is below. It also is the place where you can connect with the Tao and through which your essence can come forth. It is the body's love center, as opposed to the second chakra, which is about sexuality, creativity, and emotions.

You would focus your awareness on your solar plexus if you were interested in working more kinetically. If, for example, you were interacting with an assailant, you would center yourself in the third chakra to bring your kinetic power into play.

The crown chakra is the center for universal connection. How is this different from the heart chakra? Your heart, you might say, is a direct route to the Tao, which is the universe's source. Through your crown there is the weaving of connection with everything that emanates from the Tao. That includes other souls on all planes as well as the elements.

The eighth and ninth chakras, incidentally, begin the process of stepping down higher energies so that the physical body can handle them. Actually, you could see each chakra as stepping down the frequency of the emanation from the next higher chakra. Chakra energies become denser as they go farther down into the body.

*What about the third eye and solar plexus as connections to the Tao?*

The third eye is the seat of perception. The solar plexus works with personal power. The sun is the source of light and heat—power—for the earth. Every person is like a miniature sun. Through your solar plexus, you radiate your own personal sunlight. The heart chakra is a window of pure, neutral Tao energy.

*Is the heart chakra the only place one can connect directly to the Tao?*

Within the limitations of semantics, we would say yes. However, another way of looking at it is that everything in the universe is contained within the Tao. Everything is part of it, springs from it, and is it.

*What about, for instance, yogis who specialize in one of the chakras, not the heart chakra? Would you say that they are not connected to the Tao?*

We do not wish to promote a hierarchy among the chakras. Each is equal in importance and value. One does not obtain enlightenment through one chakra above another. If you feel moved to work with a particular chakra more than the others, that is probably appropriate for you. What is right for one person is not necessarily right for another.

*How can you tell if your chakras are functioning properly? If they're not, what can you do about it?*

There are many practices designed to open and attune the chakras. You can use visualizations, sound, chanting, gemstones, and many other tools. The key is your intent that it occur, and making space for it to happen. Everything seeks health and balance. If you give it the space, it will move in that direction. A good approach is simply to bring your attention to one particular chakra, ask that it be cleared, and observe the process while it occurs. But any method comfortable for you is fine.

You can assume that if you have not been giving them specific attention, they need some, just as a car needs its oil changed periodically. When you live in a place that is highly polluted, both physically and psychically, you need to clean your chakras more often. Spending five minutes a day working with your chakras can do much toward keeping them healthy and attuned once they are basically functioning well.

*If a person has an illness in an area of the body near a particular chakra, would giving that chakra extra attention be helpful? Is there a relationship between it and the illness?*

Usually there is, and extra attention to the nearest chakra can be useful. You can communicate directly with it. For example, if you have a headache, you might bring your awareness to brow chakra and ask what you are holding there, what emotion or belief might be contributing to the headache.

*If the fourth chakra is central, not the second, why are emotions, which relate more to the second chakra, always portrayed as being so compelling?*

People often mistake second chakra infatuation with heart chakra love. They glamorize infatuation partly because there is little evidence of mature love around. Not knowing their own hearts, they assume that infatuation is about as good as it gets. Immediate emotion is all they know. Emotions are important and should not be repressed, but they are not the whole self. In the heart, the whole self comes together. To know your heart, you must spend time there.

*Would you say that being romantically in love is a combination of fourth and second chakra energy?*

Yes. We would define being in love as a state of bonding both at the personal (second chakra) and impersonal (fourth chakra) levels; in other words, you love someone both emotionally and spiritually, both subjectively and objectively, in both your immediate reaction and your overall response. Body-type attraction, emotional triggering, karmic ties, and even essence contact (transcendentally connecting with the soul) alone are not the same as being in love.

## 16 • CRYSTALS AND GEMSTONES

As with chakras, crystals and gemstones are well covered in other texts, but here are some brief comments on them.

*I was using rose quartz to help stay in my body. I wore two double-strand anklets of it. Was that necessary, or would a small chip in my pocket have done the same thing?*

Stones around your ankles would tend to draw energy farther into the body than one in your pocket.

*Would one stone on the ankle have been just as effective as a string of them?*

Probably not, because several stones have more volume. In general, larger or more stones will influence a greater area, and clearer stones will do it with more intensity or in less time. Also, by circling your ankles, you were demonstrating that you wished to have a complete experience of being in your body. A circle is like a circuit. Stones, of course, have inherent energies, but the way they are used is also symbolic. When you make a symbol such as two circular anklets, you place in your subconscious a command, just as when you take vitamins. Vitamins have nutritional value, but taking them is also a symbol that says to your body, "Get well," or "Be healthy." One stone in your pocket still has both symbolic and energetic value, but probably not as much.

A stone's ability to receive and give energy partly depends on how vibrationally clean it is. It may be powerful, but if it is full of dirty energies it has pulled off you or the environment, it loses effectiveness. Stones should be cleansed more often than most people realize. Twice a week would not be too often for those you wear or use daily, especially if you live in a polluted urban area.

The method you use for cleansing stones does not matter that much. Placing them in a clean glass jar containing distilled water and sea salt in direct sunlight is a good one. The clean water gives them a medium into which they can empty debris. Water is different from air, obviously. Stones you have been using are used to the air, so they are not necessarily going to release into it. They know that when they are in air, one of their jobs is to pull stuck energies out from it, not the reverse; thus the advantage of using salt water. Salt alone, sand, and soil also work. It is your intent that they be cleansed that counts most. It can take anywhere from half a day to a week to cleanse a stone.

*Can too large a quantity or mass of stones be harmful?*

Usually not. However, if a person who is severely imbalanced uses a powerful stone or one that is not appropriate for him, it could create movement that is too fast for him to handle. The energy itself is not destructive, but people can change only so quickly. If the stone initiates change that is too fast, it will be experienced as being negative. That is rare. Normally, a neutral stone like a clear quartz cannot be too large or too powerful. If a person sleeps on a bed over five hundred crystals, with others hanging from the ceiling and surrounding him on the floor, he may find that to be too much stimulation! With someone simply wearing, carrying, or using a stone, there is usually not a problem.

*Is a stone more effective flush against the body than merely being near it?*

If you are wearing synthetic fibers and the stone is weak, flush against the body is preferable. Nylon clothing is particularly insulating to the energies of stones. If you are wearing natural fibers and the stone is right up against the clothing, it does not make too much difference.

*How long does a stone need to be applied for optimal benefit?*

This must be intuited. It varies from stone to stone and application to application. If, for example, you are meditating with clear and strong concentration and are highly receptive, it may take only a moment to make a deep connection with the energy of a crystal and effect a change. On the other hand, if you are not very connected with yourself, or your situation is severe or not very responsive to change, it may take hours for the energy to get through. In such a case, you might want to wear or carry the stone, or affix it to your body with surgical tape. Generally, a few minutes to about half an hour of contact is sufficient for someone to receive as much of a stone's energy as he can at that time. In another half hour or half day, he may be able to receive more, so the stone could be reapplied. With a chronic health problem this could go on for some time.

To determine if the circuit has been made—in other words, if the energy has been received—simply ask the stone and you will know. The stone can also tell you if and when it should next be reapplied. Even a person who is not very experienced with either stones or intuitive work in general is usually able to know if he asks.

*If you aren't working on a particular part of the body, does it matter where you place stones? For example, if you want to work on emotions, might it be more effective to put a stone over the heart or second chakra?*

Yes, especially for symbolic purposes. People receive benefit from symbols in ways of which they are not conscious. Even if a person does not consciously know what a heart chakra is, he subliminally knows that it is the place of integration, so placing it there has significance. In terms of energy, it is a little more convenient there, but it could go anywhere near the body and be of benefit.

*How powerful is the energy of stones compared with other factors that affect one?*

Stones work primarily on a spiritual level rather than directly with surface manifestations. Clearing and strengthening your energies can heal you, especially if your problem is primarily spiritual to begin with, and you are ready and willing to change. At least, that can contribute to healing along with other approaches. Using crystals with nutritional changes, herbs, homeopathy, and emotional and psychological work is an example of supporting healing from many directions.

*Suppose that someone is in an inherently agitating circumstance, and he is using a stone to calm himself, what are the relative potencies of those two influences?*

For most people, a strong crystal would not be as much of an influence as a strong negative external circumstance, but it would provide some aid in coping with the circumstance. It would depend on just how intense the outer circumstances are, how powerful the stone is, and how responsive the person is to spiritual energies. Some people find the right stone to be a very calming influence. Others are more open to environmental influences; for them the balance is tilted the other way.

*Are natural or cut crystals better for healing, wearing, and programming?*

Cutting a crystal can have either a positive or negative effect. Sometimes cutting the crystal helps focus or free its energies. For example, perhaps there is a natural flow in the piece, and there is some debris on the side that is blocking this flow. Delicately removing it can intensify the crystal's energy. It would require a high level of perception on the part of the one doing the cutting to perceive these energy flows. He would also need to know how to work with the crystal rather than against it.

Cut crystals have a reduced energy about ninety percent of the time. Sometimes the reduction is negligible; sometimes it is major. Of course, cutting may make a crystal more aesthetically pleasing, either visually or to the touch. This may be worth a slight reduction in energy. After all, there may still be plenty of energy in it. If the cutting violates its flow, it can cripple its usefulness. Perhaps half of the cut crystals you might run across have this problem. On the other hand, an uncut or natural crystal may also be of little use because it simply does not have much native power. A good crystal that is sensitively cut is better than a mediocre crystal that is natural. Nonetheless, uncut crystals are usually preferable for most healing applications unless you need a crystal with a focused or directed energy flow, rather than one that radiates in all directions. Some natural crystals are focused, but cut crystals more often tend to be focused.

For programming, the key is not whether the crystal is cut or uncut, but its clarity.

For wearing, it would depend on the particular stone and why you are wearing it. Is it for healing? Are you wearing it because you have programmed it to bring you abundance? Or is it mostly decorative? Your purpose in wearing it determines whether cut or uncut is preferable.

## 17 • NUTRITION FOR THE ILL

When a person's body is highly toxic, there is little room for nourishment. If the body's energy is occupied with digesting food, it does not have the opportunity to detoxify. So normally, a lack of appetite should be respected—the body knows what it needs. Hunger usually returns when the toxins are adequately eliminated.

When there has been medical intervention, however, the body's impulses may be confused and unreliable. Also, when a person is exhausted, she may not have the energy to eat and digest much food, which can form a vicious circle leading to greater depletion. In such a case, it may be worthwhile to persuade her to eat more, especially foods that are easily assimilated, such as fresh, raw vegetable and fruit juices.

When administering vitamins, minerals, herbs, and so forth to someone ill, it can be valuable to say something about their specific healing properties as a kind of affirmation. The substances work without your doing that because they instruct the body in a chemical language the body understands, but such affirmations potentize them. It is also a way of joining forces with the person to reinforce her healing intent.

The body's need for nutritional substances is constantly changing. Ideally, rather than following fixed dosages, you would intuitively check the person to see what she needs at any given time. Applied kinesiology, pendulum work, or simply asking within while using your own body to mirror hers, can be used. It is difficult, however, to receive intuitive instructions clearly if you are physically, emotionally, and/or mentally unclear, especially if you lack experience with such techniques. In that case, you might want to consult someone experienced who can get the information more accurately and easily than you can. If such a person is not available daily, it is all right to follow fixed dosages until new information is available.

Meanwhile, you can practice developing your perception. Stop and sense her body, the tablets, and yourself. See if you can perceive whether two or three tablets, for instance, would be more appropriate.

## 18 • HEALING AFFIRMATIONS

The following are affirmations that promote healing. There can be value in working with them whether or not you view yourself as physically healthy, because you are constantly creating health—it is not a destination at which you can arrive.

Even if you recognize these statements as ultimate truths, they may not presently be factual for you. By repeating them to yourself—aloud, silently, or in writing—you can make them so for yourself. If you do not feel them but would like to, express them as if you do feel them, as an actor might. Thought often precedes feeling, and the purpose of affirmations is to deliberately change your thoughts. The more conviction with which you express them, the better they will "take." If you do not intellectually believe what you are affirming, see the affirmation as an experiment: "What would happen if I took this attitude?" You are trying it on for size, so to speak, seeing if it has a positive effect. If it does, you may choose to believe it, since an affirmation can only heal to the degree that it is true. Even if you are consciously skeptical, an appropriate affirmation will help if you do it properly.

Many of those listed here are similar, but each one has a different effect due to its precise wording. Some affirmations also have alternative wordings within them, which are in parentheses. You can try all of them that seem applicable, noting those to which you respond the most deeply (those that feel the best, or that trigger the greatest reaction in you). You can then do further work with those. Note any negative thoughts that arise; rather than repressing them, lovingly delve more deeply into them, letting yourself understand the reasons for them, until they no longer come up when you state those affirmations. You may wish to devise affirmations that directly address what is coming up in you. You may also wish to state them from

## HEALING AFFIRMATIONS

different parts of yourself—for example, from your feet, head, heart, and from yourself as if you were a large orb. Be creative. You may wish to record yourself reciting them, and play them back to yourself as you go to sleep or take walks, for instance. Reciting them aloud may amplify them for you. Do not be afraid to improvise on them. Use them until they no longer elicit a response in you, either positive or negative.

If you are working with someone else, you can use affirmations in the second and third person. For example, after he says, "I am love," you might say, "You are love" or "He or she (using the person's name) is love."

*I am the healing force.*

*I trust in the movement of love.*

*I release myself (my family, my friends* [can name them individually]*) into the hands of love.*

*I am the love in all things.*

*I have no need to hold onto anything because I am the love in all things.*

*It is safe for me to let go of all worry and just reveal the love that I am.*

*It is okay for me just to be.*

*I let go of all responsibility except the responsibility to be love.*

*I trust in the power of love to heal my body.*

*I trust in the love given to me by my doctors (family, friends, etc.) to help my body heal itself.*

## OPENING TO HEALING

*I let go of all worry about the future, knowing that as I yield to love, the very best things possible will happen.*

*I have no need to worry about anyone or anything. I can just be.*

*When I feel afraid, I love my fear.*

*When I feel anxious, I love my anxiety.*

*When I start to feel that I need to be in control, I love my feeling that I need to be in control.*

*I am not afraid of any of my feelings. I love all my feelings.*

*All my feelings are trying to help me get well. I include them in love so that I may truly get well.*

*I am thankful for all the opportunities I have to learn the lessons of love.*

*I find it easier and easier each day to let go and just be love.*

*I let go of all worry about what I should or should not do, and simply let myself know what is right for me to do moment by moment.*

*I know that I am being guided and that I cannot do the wrong thing.*

*I let the power of love heal me.*

*I no longer need to be in control of my healing process.*

*The more I let go, the more powerful I am.*

*I can relax about everything that has been worrying me, and enjoy the process of healing.*

# HEALING AFFIRMATIONS

*The more I let go, the more alive I am.*

*The more I let go, the healthier I am.*

*I trust my body's urge to heal. I don't have to make it get well. All I have to do is support it.*

*I am becoming healthier every day.*

*As I yield to love, my body feels better and better.*

*I now release all negative thoughts I've picked up from others (through my medical treatment, etc.).*

*I allow new life to move in my heart* [can name any area needing healing].

*I receive the energy of my essence.*

*Each cell of my body receives the healing light of my essence.*

*I now let go to my inner healing source.*

*I am my healing power.*

*I am my healing source.*

*I receive healing energy into the top of my head* [can name any other body part].

*I receive healing energy into my fear* [can name any other emotion].

*I am my power in my hands* [can name any other body part].

*I receive healing.*

## OPENING TO HEALING

*I deserve to be healed.*

*I deserve to feel perfectly well.*

*I am as capable of receiving healing as anyone else.*

*Love and light are with me always.*

*I am eternally safe in the light.*

*I am always with the light.*

*The light is always with me.*

*I am the light.*

*I ask that the divine, universal spirit bring total healing into my life.*

*It is now safe for me to open to love.*

*I ask that the perfect pattern for my body come forth.*

*I feel the energy of the perfect spiritual pattern for my body.*

*I allow the energy of my perfect spiritual pattern to increase.*

*I receive perfect health into my physical body.*

*I fully let go of all old, negative patterns for my physical body.*

*I let go of all negative ideas about my body.*

*The perfect pattern for my body is always available.*

*No matter what symptoms I manifest, I am increasing my*

# HEALING AFFIRMATIONS

*health.*

*I let healing come from the perfect spiritual pattern for my physical body.*

*I find it easy to let go.*

*I no longer need to clench.*

*It feels so good to let go and relax.*

*I am now fully supported from within.*

*I no longer experience myself as hanging off a cliff. I am on solid ground; therefore, I can let go.*

*I give the perfect spiritual pattern for my body a full opportunity to come forth.*

*I relax into the perfect spiritual pattern for my body.*

*I continue to receive the energy coming forth from the perfect spiritual pattern for my body.*

*I am the healing energy of my soul.*

*I receive my perfect spiritual pattern for my chest* [can name any other body part].

*I am a magnificent, radiant being.*

*I am light.*

*I allow my body to receive more fully the light of who I am.*

*I allow my struggle and resistance to receive the light of who I am.*

*I am the light that created my body and that now recreates*

## OPENING TO HEALING

it.

*I am the light of total and absolute love manifested in my body.*

*I am the love that assuages all my fears.*

*I no longer have to struggle.*

*I open to my healing power twenty-four hours a day.*

*I give my healing power full permission to heal my body.*

*My healing power is healing me even when I'm doubting it.*

*I now allow myself to stay focused on receiving healing energy, even in the presence of painful symptoms.*

*I receive healing energy directly into all areas of need.*

*My pain is a reminder to open to healing energy.*

*I continue to receive healing power.*

*I am receiving healing in all that I do.*

*I now know that I am the source of healing for my body.*

*I am harmonious.*

*I receive energy.*

*I receive health.*

*I am the source of my health.*

*I receive love.*

*I receive love in my head* [can name any other body part].

## HEALING AFFIRMATIONS

*I release myself into love.*

*I accept my anger.*

*I love my anger.*

*I accept my frustration.*

*I love my frustration.* (You cannot go past your frustration, but you can go through it. Love your frustration and it will change. There is power in acceptance and love. If you battle your frustration, it will entrench itself.)

*I open to my frustration.*

*It is all right for me to feel angry and frustrated.*

*I relax into my anger and frustration.*

*I love and accept my body exactly the way it is, just as a mother loves and accepts her child exactly the way he (she) is.*

*Healing flows from my love and acceptance of my body.*

*Healing flows to my body in the presence of my anger and frustration.*

*Healing flows to my body no matter what I do or do not do.*

*My body is learning to relax in the presence of pain.*

*My body is learning to breathe freely in the presence of pain.*

*My body is learning to breathe freely all the time.*

*There is no need to fight or struggle with anything.*

## OPENING TO HEALING

*When I begin to fight or struggle, I remember to relax.*

*It is easy for me to relax completely.*

*It is easy for me to receive the healing power of love.*

*I acknowledge love as the fundamental energy of life.*

*I acknowledge love as the most powerful force in the universe.*

*Every cell of my body is receiving love.*

*Love is already a reality. I continue to open to it more and more.*

*I acknowledge the reduction of pain in my body.*

*I thank my body for opening to love in a greater way.*

*I allow my arms* [can name any other body part] *to open to love in a greater way.*

*I fully let go to love in my arms* [can name any other body part].

*I open to love (peace, etc.) with my whole being.*

*I let go of struggle.*

*I let go to the love I am.*

*My symptoms are parts of me crying out for my love.*

*Whenever I feel pain I respond with total love.*

*Whenever I feel frustrated (angry, etc.) with my pain, I respond with love to my frustration as well as to my pain.*

# HEALING AFFIRMATIONS

*I am learning to see love all around me.*

*All the people around me are embodiments of love.*

*Since love is the source of healing, I see all the people who love me as sources of healing.*

*All the plants (animals, minerals, objects, etc.) around me are embodiments of love and therefore sources of healing.*

*I feel my bed as an embodiment of love and a source of healing.*

*The air I breathe is an embodiment of love and a source of healing.*

*I trust love.*

*I am love.*

*I am the power of love.*

*I am the healing power of love.*

*I fill my whole space with love.*

*I am healing my body all the time.*

*I am healing my body even when my symptoms are evident.*

*I am healing my body even when I am in pain.*

*I am healing my body even when it appears otherwise.*

*I am healing every cell of my body at every moment of my life.*

*Opening to love sets me free.*

## OPENING TO HEALING

*I feel the presence of healing energy in my body.*

*Love is now healing my back* [can name any other body part].

*I am the healing power that relaxes my throat* [can name any other body part].

*I am the relaxation that heals my body.*

*I deserve to receive the healing power of love completely.*

*I have total confidence in my ability to receive the healing power of love.*

*I have everything it takes to heal completely.*

*I put total trust in the healing power of love.*

*Everything I do brings healing for me.*

*I commit to fully and continually opening to my healing energy in my thoughts.*

*The life energy that created my body is now recreating it.*

*I trust the life that brings me aliveness to expand my aliveness in my body.*

*In love, I embrace life.*

*I need not cling to life in desperation. I trust life, and know that it is always there for me. Therefore, I simply relax.*

*I embrace life heartily through the food I eat.*

*Because my body is becoming more peaceful, relaxed, and open, I am able to eat more food each day.*

# HEALING AFFIRMATIONS

*I am now comfortably accepting more and more nourishment into my body.*

*I have always been spiritually advanced enough to open to healing and to bring greater health to my body. I forgive myself for not realizing this before. I am beginning to know this now, and I am thankful for that.*

*Whenever I speak the loving truth, I feel better. I am learning to speak the truth in my thoughts and words always.*

*It is easy for me to remember to speak the loving truth about my body and about everything else in my life.*

*The truth sets me free to be more fully who I already am.*

*I am already love, truth, life, health, joy, peace, and happiness.*

*I find it easy to accept my condition exactly the way it is right now, because I know that it is the perfect starting point for creating health.*

*I use however I feel as a starting point to create health.*

*I know that healing power is always present in my body, even when I cannot discern it.*

*I love and accept the parts of me that are skeptical or negative. They are perfect starting points for healing. I open to healing in the presence of my skepticism and negativity, just as I open to healing in the presence of my pain and discomfort.*

*I need no special circumstances to open to healing. I open to healing whether it is noisy or quiet. I open to healing whether I am fatigued or energetic. I open to healing even while others around me are fearful and negative.*

*The more strongly that others believe I will not recover, the more my healing would inspire and bless them; therefore, I do not mind their negativity. I enjoy showing them that they, too, can open to their healing power.*

*I joyfully anticipate fun things I am going to do when I have more strength. I also take full advantage of how things are now to enjoy myself. I listen to music that is pleasurable and healing. I enjoy life-affirming movies, inspiring reading, and other activities available to me now. Most of all, I cherish this golden opportunity to come to better know my beautiful self.*

*I let the river inside me flow.*

*I let the river inside me carry away all that does not belong.*

*I allow the river inside me to carry away all the pain in my body (my headache, the tumors, etc.)*

*I allow myself to feel the river inside me more fully.*

*I open to the river inside me in the face of pain.*

*The river inside me is carrying away my pain (cancer, etc.); I don't need it anymore.*

*I let go of my pain (cancer, etc.).*

*I let go of all sickness in my body; I don't need it anymore.*

*I let go of all confusion in my body; I don't need it anymore.*

*I let go of all fear in my body; I don't need it anymore.*

# HEALING AFFIRMATIONS

*The river of love carries away all fear from my body.*

*I trust my power.*

*I dare to be love.*

*I acknowledge my letting go.*

*I am the letting go.*

*I continue letting go.*

*I now allow my essence to come forth fully and fill my space.*

*I now allow my essence to burn away any residues of what does not belong.*

*As I let go of what does not belong, I feel lighter and lighter.*

*I allow love to come forth and fill my whole space.*

*I am the love that fills my space.*

*I include my anger (darkness, hate, shortcomings, etc.) in my love.*

*I forgive myself.*

*I forgive the part of myself that makes mountains out of molehills (is self-indulgent, feels helpless, etc.)*

*I include in my love the part of myself that feels powerless.*

*I am ready to let go.*

*I release my fear of letting go.*

## OPENING TO HEALING

*I let go.*

*I am whole.*

*I am the harmony of my wholeness.*

*I open to my harmony now.*

*I release my fear of harmony.*

*I reestablish harmony.*

*I allow myself to be fully in harmony.*

*I am at peace with my harmony.*

*I let go of all my limiting concepts about myself.*

*I open to my essence.*

*I now reclaim my life.*

# Part IV

# BECOMING WELL

## 19 • PURGING

When one cycle ends and another begins, there is a process of purging what is no longer needed. In gardening, after the harvest, you might prepare the soil for the next season by plowing under the waste from the one just ended. The stalks, husks, leaves, and so forth break down, providing necessary elements for the next cycle of growth. You might also need to remove rocks, dead branches, and other matter too dense to break down by the next season. In a relatively new garden, there is likely to be a good deal of such matter.

During this soil preparation, the value of your labors is not immediately apparent. However, if you were to plant next spring in rocky, branch-laden, and infertile soil, your harvest would be diminished. Once spring comes, you might need to do further work on the soil before planting to deal with changes that occurred over the winter.

There is also an internal purging process that is more active during endings and beginnings. It occurs on all levels of self, not just in the conscious mind, so you are not consciously aware of all that is being purged. That is just as well—otherwise you might get in the way. If you were cleaning out a closet, your progress would be hampered if you could not let go of things, if you habitually reasoned, "This is a perfectly good whatever, and in thirty years' time it will be an antique," or "I may need that someday." You might never notice it if your partner cleaned out the closet and you did not know that he had disposed of those items. So it is well that much internal purging is unconscious.

The purging process sometimes triggers survival fears. You may recall when something aided you in some way that you associated with your survival, so you hold onto it. But when you get rid of things no longer of use to you, whether internally or externally, it gives you more room to breathe and makes what is valuable to you more accessible—it actually supports your survival.

A certain amount of purging is automatic. If your physical body is reasonably healthy, dead cells and other waste are eliminated constantly while new cells are created. However, due to poor diet, lack of exercise, inadequate water, pollution, and so on, not everything that is toxic or no longer needed is necessarily eliminated. Most people's bodies are clogged to some degree; wastes are not fully free to be flushed out, so they stay in the body. Vitality is reduced because the body has to carry that waste in addition to its normal functions. Sometimes it gets sick just to push out some of this excess. If there had been a conscious choice to support the body's automatic purging process with changes in diet and so forth, becoming sick may not have been necessary. Such support can allow purging to be more complete and effective. The same is true of purging at higher levels.

Much intellectual and emotional purging also occurs automatically as a result of the natural operation of thought and feeling. You may have been upset by yesterday's traffic jam or a comment your boss made to you, but you have likely forgotten it by now. Just as your body can become clogged, however, excess stress or events that are too large or important for this normal elimination process can clog your psyche. In that case, you need to take deliberate steps to support the natural purging process. It is like changing your diet or exercise to help your body purge when it is clogged.

Most people carry intellectual and emotional debris from past lives. Not everything that is troubling a person can necessarily be attributed to a painful childhood or other events in the current lifetime.

The most significant of these psyche-clogging events are traumas, upsets you see as threats to your survival that you do not yet know how to handle. You stuff them into the closet of your psyche, just as you might stuff items you do not know what to do with into your closets. Sometimes you open your psychic closet door and everything comes tumbling out. Nothing more can be stuffed in. Your psyche says, "Lighten the load. I cannot carry this weight any longer."

Occasional concentrated periods of purging—eliminating the old—are a normal part of life. When your closets are stuffed with more than they are designed to handle, illness of some kind may occur. The degree to which your purging is painful and confusing is the degree to which you have not been keeping your closets in order all along.

You cannot fully cleanse traumas from yourself unconsciously. By definition, a trauma is an event that is too much for you to handle, something you postpone dealing with. It remains incomplete in you until you are ready to take responsibility for it, recognizing and finishing whatever is unfinished. It is comparable to a log on a compost pile; although some of its surface may rot, it will not adequately break down in time for the next growing season if you do not take responsibility for it and saw it into manageable pieces. To go back to the analogy of cleaning out your closet, it is an item that is too heavy for your partner (your unconscious mind) to carry out alone. It requires both of you working together.

Suppose that when you were a child, you were made fun of because of your physical appearance. If you experienced that as trauma—in other words, if you were not able to deal with it successfully at the time—you put it in your psychic closet. If you find yourself thinking about it now for some reason, this is an indication that you are ready to deal with it. Every time you open the closet door, it falls on the ground with a thud, and you are reminded of it.

Every trauma has its own requirements for healing. Ask the traumatized part of yourself what it needs, and draw upon your highest insight and wisdom in meeting those needs. Hopefully, you have learned enough between the trauma and the purging to do what is required. If not, you might seek counseling.

The purging of trauma occurs by knowing the truth about it. The truth releases all that is not free. Knowing the truth is not just having intellectual understanding—it is having emotional compassion as well. There may be a need to cry tears that were not cried before, or to cry them again with compassion and understanding rather than fear.

Healing trauma leads to much growth for the soul. That you were traumatized in the first place indicates that there was a part of you that did not know the truth. If you were traumatized by other children making fun of your physical appearance, you did not fully love or accept yourself as you were. It is understandable that you would be hurt by their unkindness. Nevertheless, if you have self-confidence and are at ease with yourself (which comes from loving yourself), people are less like to make unkind remarks to you. If they do, you are able to disregard them as meaningless to you.

Such maturity does not come gratis. One does not start out being this together, as they say. Traumas are actually part of the way you become together. Fully realized people cannot be traumatized, but they are very rare. You can probably still be traumatized in one way or another, and that is all right. That is part of your humanity. You and your fellows can help one another learn your lessons and heal your hurts.

It is possible to grow and evolve without traumas, although we know of no one who has evolved without them completely. This is growing through joy rather than pain. As you walk the spiritual path, your traumas and other difficulties tend to decrease, and your joys increase.

Nevertheless, there are times when you feel the need to work on what you have not completed in the past. You can support your purging simply by making space for it: being quiet within, taking walks, meditating, eating well, sleeping more, or just keeping your life a little quieter, not putting so many other stresses on yourself that you do not have a chance to do justice to the purging. You can trust your intuitive desires for these kinds of activities.

When healing, it is important to allow whatever wishes to come up to do so. Do not judge anything you feel. See yourself as a scientist exploring your inner realm. You are seeking to discover what is there and what is needed. Be detached from what is happening in the sense of not overly identifying with it. At the same time, allow the waves of inner movement to flow freely, so that if you feel a desire to move your body, make a sound, or express a feeling, you can do so.

Keeping a journal during periods of intense purging can help you be with yourself. Receiving support from others can help you know that you are not alone in what you are going through, that others experience similar things and that you can help each other. If you work with a group, its energy can intensify the cleansing and make it easier.

Ultimately, purging occurs because of your essence's longing to come forth more fully. If you think that you *are* what is being purged, you will not let go. If you align with your essence and let spiritual force move in the way it wants to, the purging will be much easier.

## MEDITATION

Bring your awareness to your first (root) chakra, at the base of your spine. Let it open like a drain emptying into a "compost heap" in the earth.

Let your crown chakra open. Feel a steady stream of energy entering it and filling your body. Let it flow out through your root chakra into the earth, carrying away all debris. It is like being washed through with sparkling clean water.

# PURGING

As you feel the energy streaming through you, repeat to yourself the following affirmations. If you feel a shift when you say one, remember it—it will probably help you later. Check from time to time to see if the process is open and flowing. Notice your root chakra; feel yourself letting the energy pour out into the earth. Check around your heart; feel that you are letting go. Be aware of your crown; feel that you are receiving. Make sure that your breathing is relaxed.

*I am safe.*

*It is safe for me to release completely.*

*I love myself wholeheartedly, no matter what I have done or not done in the past.*

*I am at peace with the process of purging in myself.*

*I am now willing to experience and heal my pain from the past.*

*I now receive love and help in my cleansing process.*

*All my feelings are good. I embrace them.*

*All my loved ones support me in my healing.*

*The entire universe supports me in my healing and growth. I am never alone.*

*I allow energy to flow freely in me always.*

*I can easily let go of the old because the new is always abundantly available to me.*

Keep feeling the energy draining out into the earth. Feel a magnetic force in the center of the earth pulling it from you so it is effortless on your part. All you have to do is relax and let it flow.

*I find it easy to let go in the purging process.*

*I no longer resist cleansing. I love letting go of the old and receiving the new.*

Take a moment to check yourself out. See where you are in your purging cycle and quietly be with yourself. Ask how you can best continue to support this process.

# 20 • RECOVERING

*[To Specific Individuals]*

## MOTIVATION

You would be wise to think more clearly about why you wish to heal. You are now primarily trying to escape pain. You would progress more quickly if you were instead embracing joy. Joy need not wait until after your healing—it can actually bring healing.

## BELIEFS

As an experiment, we suggest that for a couple of days you stop thinking about what is going to happen, whether the doctors are right or wrong, and so forth. Instead, put your focus on listening to yourself. Notice your beliefs, and other people's beliefs that you carry. Start making decisions about whether you want to carry them anymore. What you believe is important.

## DISCOMFORT

It is said that it is darkest before the dawn. Usually, it feels worse before the catharsis that initiates the final stages of healing. It is also said not to judge a book by its cover. People tend to think that anything uncomfortable is bad and anything that feels pleasant is good. Chocolate layer cake tastes pleasant whereas fish liver oil does not, yet who can judge which will ultimately bring more benefit?

Everyone's path is different. What you need to go through to heal is unique. That is partly why judging things as being good or bad is not useful. Your process is perfect for you, as everyone else's is for him.

## CHANGING BODY CONSCIOUSNESS

You are learning to assist your body consciousness in assimilating new patterns. It is as if you had divorced and remarried, and were guiding your young child through that transition. You have divorced your negative patterns of thought and are marrying more positive ones. Your body, like a child, is confused, and has not fully accepted the changes. As you maintain your mental clarity and stay connected with your body consciousness, it is inevitable that it will align with your new awareness.

## SLEEP

It is not uncommon for someone processing trauma to require more sleep. It is strenuous work and depletes the body.

When you sleep, an ascension process set in motion during the day, raising your vibration, can continue on deeper levels.

## BURNOUT

Your body and psyche tell you what they need. If you have gotten to the point of burnout, you have not been listening to their messages, or if you have, you have not acted on them.

You are the most important thing you have. If you do not take care of yourself, you cannot go out and get another one!

## IMBALANCE

Generally, disease does not cause imbalance—it merely highlights it.

## 21 • REBALANCING

### [*To Someone Feeling Unwell*]

Your health is better than you think it is. You are healing unfinished business not only from this lifetime but from others as well. You have to be strong to be able to do this. Your essence would not be bringing these imbalances to the surface if you were not healthy enough to process them. Some people become sick when their bodies are so overloaded that they can no longer carry the imbalances, which then spill out in disease. When these diseases are not survived, the spilling out is still healing spiritually. In your case, your essence is bringing forth these imbalances not because it has to but because it can. Once they are cleared away, your level of function will be higher than it was previously. We are not merely referring to more physical energy but to a new level of spiritual force. Your body could not have sustained an increased spiritual force previously because of its latent imbalances, even when you appeared to be relatively healthy.

Were you not flushing out these imbalances, eventually they would cause your body to break down in a serious disease, either in this or a future lifetime, which would be much more difficult to heal. The symptoms you feel now, however, are almost the same as if that were happening, although your pain and discomfort are less now because you have not let it go to that extreme. You should view and take care of yourself like a person who is healing a serious disease, so that you are not surprised or upset if, for instance, you occasionally feel weak. While your body is rebalancing, do not expect it to function the same way it does when it is balanced.

One activity that can benefit you in the rebalancing process is light exercise. It should feel pretty good to you.

If you were truly ill, you would not be able to handle even light exercise. Since you have the strength, light exercise can help you keep your momentum going so that your body does not become bogged down in any particular rebalancing. That happens sometimes if the purging process weakens the body beyond its capacity to handle the rebalancing.

Your imbalances stem from childhood and past-life traumas. Trauma is damage that occurs to a part of you that is not strong enough to meet a challenge. Like a physical injury, it tends to become a weak link in the chain and is especially susceptible to further injury until it is strengthened and rebalanced. Had you been strong in those parts of yourself to begin with, they might not have been traumatized in the first place. You tested them and found them to be weak. Now you are taking time out to process those traumas, purging the negative energies they generated in you, healing and strengthening the parts of you that experienced them, and rebalancing your whole system around these changes. This takes time and energy.

The more trauma you have had in a particular area, the more it can become one of your greatest strengths once you heal it—through so much experience, you become an "expert" in it. When you have strengthened all aspects of yourself so that you cannot be easily traumatized in any area, you can end your time on the physical plane. You might say that the physical plane is a health spa for the soul, helping you get the various parts of yourself in shape.

When you experience trauma in weak aspects of yourself and then strengthen them, you are growing through pain. You can also grow through joy, by consciously seeing what is weak and strengthening it without having to be alerted to that weakness by pain. Few people use growing through joy as their predominant method. You are learning how to do this. However, if you needed to grow through pain in the past, that is all right.

# REBALANCING

You can forgive yourself for your lack of consciousness.

You think that you have to get over this period of unwellness as quickly as possible so that you can move on and have the growth experiences you want, but you are already growing a great deal. Right now, these are your most important growth experiences. The hardest part of them—the experience of the traumas in the first place—is well behind you. Healing the traumas, strengthening the parts of you that experienced them, and rebalancing yourself is not nearly as difficult, but it does take time, especially when you are handling several. Rather than focusing on how much trauma you are dealing with, you might emphasize how strong you are becoming. Everything you are doing right now—physically, psychologically, emotionally, and spiritually—fits together and contributes to your process. Although you feel stalled in getting on with your life because you often do not feel well, nothing you are experiencing is wasted. Opening to higher energies, though, can accelerate your process. It is like putting gas in your tank. Your worry and anxiety are a waste of energy. They do not stop the process, but they are a drag on it. They are like static on a radio broadcast that does not stop you from hearing it, but makes you enjoy it less.

Let go of worry and anxiety, and enjoy and trust your process. You have plenty of time to do everything. If you recognize that what you are doing now is your highest priority, you can accept with good graces that your plans have been postponed for a while. This does not mean that you are not moving forward—you move forward in the fastest possible way when you clearly perceive and act on your priorities. You are allowing the lessons of past traumas to be brought to bear so that you will not have to repeat them. You will now be strong where you were previously weak. When you recognize what is happening, the benefits of the process are obvious.

## 22 • FINDING A REASON TO LIVE

*[To Someone Exhausted]*

You are going through a stage of examining your life purpose and premises. Until this time of questioning, you were pretty much motivated by the survival urge. You kept moving because you had to, often carrying heavy weights that you took for granted. You are no longer motivated by this fear-based urge, which is mainly fear of dying, but you have not yet found a new motivation for putting one step in front of the other. So in essence, you have no motivation. This is positive because it allows what is present in you to emerge: the exhaustion of your whole self is surfacing. This is not a new condition; it has been there for some time.

To regenerate, you need to create a clear field in which energy can stay in your body and rebuild. You need to contain your energy rather than constantly using it for other people or projects. Meditation is an excellent way to contain energy. It is like damming a river and soaking in it. Avail yourself of healing practices that can pour energy into your body, such as a massage from someone of high consciousness, and any of the energy processes, such as Reiki. You can also ask for your mate's support in helping energize your body through conscious enfoldment of it. Be willing to receive energy from him and others. Visualize yourself as a large, porous fabric sculpture, absorbing regenerative energy from the universe, like a sponge that is bone dry until it is placed in the ocean. Feel each cell soak in universal power. Think of yourself as being loved by the All.

Rest and regeneration can include such activities as holding another person, spending time with animals, being outside when the weather is pleasant, and making something with your hands. Give some thought to what

# FINDING A REASON TO LIVE

sounds restful to you. To sleep more deeply, spend time before retiring doing activities that will support that, such as light stretching, taking a few deep breaths, and clearing your mind of worry. Finding something to be glad about would be especially helpful.

Your healing is not primarily about your body itself; it is about your finding a purpose to live. Why do you want to live? What do you wish to do with your life? Do not give this a quick answer. If someone were to give you ten million dollars with the proviso that you do something worthwhile with it, you would give it some thought. Think about this in the same way. Once you have a reason or reasons to live, you will begin to be differently motivated. You will begin to respond not to the whip of fear but to the song that emanates from within you.

## 23 • CHANGING THE BODY'S IMPRINT

*[To Someone with a Degenerative Disease]*

Your health problem is a challenge you can successfully handle. You chose it as a means of repaying a karmic debt. Had your belief systems been different, you might have done it differently. You chose the tried and true method of learning unconsciously through pain. This is not wrong, just painful. Few people have mastered the karmic wheel to the point that they can pay back karmic debts with awareness and joy. Now the karma has been repaid and the lesson achieved, but your body has a firm imprint—this is its reality. You must give it another reality.

Your path to healing will be primarily through consciousness. The nutritional and other physical approaches are supportive of healing. They provide raw materials for your body to use in healing. Any approach that gives your body more energy, whether it be the laying on of hands, acupressure, chiropractic, or body work such as Swedish massage, shiatsu, and so on, can be helpful. However, what will heal you is changing your body's imprint by going in consciousness where you have not gone before.

We suggest that you research emotional, psychological, and spiritual healing. It would be useful to learn some techniques, improvise variations on them, and invent new ones. If you establish a process in yourself, it will generate its own forward motion, and all you will have to do is stay with it. Dedicate time each day to being with yourself. Get to know those parts of yourself unknown to your conscious personality. Let old patterns unravel so that you can use what has been trapped within their confines to create living patterns.

One technique is meditation. For example, focus on your

heart, using your physical heart as a path into your inner heart. You could ask it to tell you about something it is carrying that needs healing. Allow the details to be clear and the images precise. Then let it direct you in healing it.

Suppose that it gives you an image of yourself as a child being pulled away from your parents. Your heart obviously wishes to work with feeling separated from parental protection. As you go deeper, you experience panic. Let it surface. It may manifest as shaking. Let yourself shake until the impulse subsides. Then you feel deep emptiness. Go into it, comforting the part of yourself holding the feeling. Be like a therapist to it, asking questions about what is going on. In this way, go deeper and deeper. When this process is complete, you will have released some emotions and beliefs associated with a past upset that is contributing, directly or indirectly, to your physical condition.

Suppose that when you ask your heart to tell you about something needing healing, you notice that your greatest pain at the time is in your left shoulder. Go into the core of the pain. Ask to know what it is about. You may get images or sensations. You might hear that you feel bad for the misery you brought others, and that you carry it as a burden. Explore the experience further and feel your remorse fully. When it clears, acknowledge that you have learned a lesson about this and that you will treat others appropriately now. Ask if you are ready to receive forgiveness. You may hear, "No, I can't do that. I am too bad a person." Do not gloss over this. Realize that this is an indication that there is more there that has not yet come to the surface. You might say, "Tell me more about this." Keep drawing it out.

If you hear, "I need to suffer more," you might ask other parts of yourself to assist you. Ask them what kinds of suffering you have already experienced. The part of you holding pain in your shoulder may not realize that its karmas have been repaid. Ask again if it will receive forgiveness. If it will not, you may simply need to give it time to process what you have learned, or you may need to explore the issue more.

Let's say that you question further, and discover that in a past life, you were very angry at someone who had ordered you to inflict suffering upon others. You wanted to stab him. However, to do so would have been fatal to you, so you held back the impulse. Freezing your shoulder to prevent yourself from stabbing him became a permanent burden because you never let the energy move, and you may also feel guilty for your anger at him. If you now let yourself safely act out the movement that you held back before, you might release it and then be willing to accept forgiveness.

Dealing with the elements of your illness is like being on an archaeological dig. You carefully shovel until you find a piece of the puzzle. You unearth it, careful not to harm it, treating it with great respect. Allow yourself to be with anything that comes up.

You have much weeping to do. Allow it. Ask for support from others. Do not feel that you must withhold it for others' benefit. You have withheld long enough. This will strengthen you, allowing you to be of even greater support for others later. It is important that you let others support you.

*Could I help change my body's imprint by doing exercises in the water that I cannot otherwise do?*

Yes. To increase your effectiveness, meditate beforehand and go into those parts of your body that believe you cannot do these exercises. Ask them to open. Promise them that you will be careful and not hurt yourself. While exercising, listen and talk with them. You might say, "See how good this feels. I am now free to move in this way. I

## CHANGING THE BODY'S IMPRINT

am now supported by life."—you can see the water as symbolizing life. "I no longer need those old patterns for my survival." Then listen.

They may say, "I might die if I move too freely." Ask why. By being creative in your exercise, you can unearth negative beliefs that would not have come up in another situation.

Use everything as a method of clearing old patterns. When you do something that indicates your strength, flexibility, safety, or anything else you wish to increase, make note of it. Acknowledge when you move more easily than usual. You might remark, "My old patterns are changing. It is easier for me to move now. Tomorrow it will be easier still. It is safe for me to move freely." Again, listen for the reply and work with it. If you do not, you might find yourself immobile the next day!

This work will prove to be worth the effort in healing not only your body but your whole being. Do not expect instant results. If you get them, fine. If you do not, enjoy the experience of getting to know yourself for as long as it takes. As you go deeper and deeper into your beliefs, you change the core instructions to your body.

## 24 • HEALING YOURSELF
*[To Specific Individuals]*

### ONE HUNDRED PERCENT COMMITMENT

Whatever course you choose, make a total commitment to open to your own healing power. You do not have to believe that you will be successful in eliminating your disease. You cannot know that in advance anyway, but that is not part of the commitment, which is simply to open to your healing power and finding out what it does. Until you have the experience, it is all theory. Knowing that someone else healed himself of an apparently fatal disease does you little good unless you find out for yourself if that is possible for you.

How do you open to your healing power? Make the commitment one hundred percent, and you will be guided. There are many techniques you can use, but techniques alone do not do the job. It is your intent to heal that is central. You will not have the intent if you do not first have the commitment.

We are not suggesting that you try to do more than you can do and overexert yourself. There are many things you can do to support your healing, and you should do everything you can. However, your commitment is not primarily to doing but to opening to your healing power, which you can let happen all the time. Out of that commitment you will naturally choose those techniques that will best support whatever your healing power is working on at any given time.

When you cut your finger and it heals, how does that happen? Does the bandage or antiseptic you put on it heal it? Who heals your finger? You do. Your healing power heals your finger, although the bandage and antiseptic support that healing. Support your healing in any way you can that feels right to you. If you listen in your heart, you will know the best way for you to do that at any given time. In addition to medical treatment, you can meditate, visualize, do affirmations, and pay attention to your breathing. You can improve your nutrition so that your healing power has more raw material. You can receive ozone therapy, acupuncture, and other holistic therapies. You can receive additional healing energy through energetic healers using techniques such as Johrei. You can work with a therapist to explore and release your blocks. You can use crystals to cleanse your atmosphere and promote conducive vibrations. Healing your body is your fulltime job at this time. You do not need to try to do everything, however, because it is not fundamentally a matter of techniques—it is a matter of opening to your healing energy in everything you do.

The reason your body is not healed now is that various things have distracted you from concentrating on your own healing energy—your pain, your fears, and so forth. That is understandable, but it is in your best interests to learn to concentrate on receiving your healing energy, even while you are undergoing medical treatment.

A strong desire to live, even if it is unconscious and is somewhat interfered with by the conscious mind, can keep a person's body alive when it otherwise would not survive. A fully conscious commitment to living is all the stronger.

You cannot expect to reach a high level of spiritual attainment overnight, but you can firmly plant yourself on the path. Struggling, trying too hard, judging yourself about not being where you want to be, and "fighting your way to the top" do not aid inner attainment; on the contrary, they get in the way. Nonetheless, full commitment is necessary.

Your primary responsibility is not first and foremost to do anything. It is to be—to be the healing source you are. It is easy to be. It is sometimes hard to do, especially when the doing does not spring from being.

See yourself as a person who is taking primary responsibility for healing herself, someone whose healing power is always flowing. For instance, when you feel pain in your arm, think of yourself as someone who is healing his arm. The opposite of that is feeling like a helpless victim, which, of course, detracts from healing.

**RESPONSIBILITY FOR LIVING**

Almost everyone has a part of himself that would rather die than accept full responsibility for living.

**THE PERFECT PATTERN**

Think of your illness as an opportunity to bring forth the perfect pattern that is present with you in spirit. Instead of focusing on what is not, develop your picture of what could be and what truly is but is not yet in manifestation. It is rather like an artist who has in mind what he wants to create, but because he has not finished, his canvas temporarily looks like a mess. When it is finished, it will be beautiful. So create a vision, an artistic vision, of what you want your body to be, which is what it already is in spirit.

Take responsibility for being the healer you are. Ultimately, everyone is a healer because everyone is a creator. Everyone participated in creating his physical body. The body is continually recreated along the lines of the consciousness held in the body.

Love is the highest reality, not the current state of one's body. Many people believe that their bodies are the only reality, and that sometimes causes them to become desperate and out of balance when they are seriously ill.

Love for yourself, for your own being, helps you open to the healing power of the love you are. Other people's love is a wonderful support, and can remind you of love, but love is really what you are. Love is the basic element of the universe, and out of that element your body was created in the first place. Love flowing freely can recreate your body into greater health. It is vital that you love your body, that you not blame it for what you have been going through. It is vital that you not feel like a victim of your body but instead take the position of the one providing the love that it needs to heal. You can easily do this.

## THE PURPOSE OF ILLNESS

Your illness is a tool you are using to heal your consciousness, to come more fully home to yourself. If you were not capable of this healing, you probably would not have manifested the illness to begin with.

Illness can be a blessing. There are people who never get a serious illness, but they are never happy because their beliefs limit them. Your illness is not an evidence of failure. It is an indication that you were ready to change your beliefs. You could no longer live with them, so you brought forth these symptoms. What was there all along became dominant, not to punish yourself but to be healed. You would not have known that you had these beliefs if something had not stopped you in your tracks.

## THE NATURE OF HEALING

The integration of positive and negative is healing. Sickness is their separation. Rather than trying to supplant negative with positive, become aware of the higher reality (positive) and let that embrace and include the lower reality (negative). Feel fully the quality of the lower (or manifest) reality in the presence of the higher. This results in a decrease in fear and an increase in love.

Working with a serious illness is difficult—it can be a very frightening lower reality. If a seriously ill person is to experience a different scenario than the one that would be inevitable if the lower reality were left on its own, she must open to the higher reality, the highest of which is love.

## OPENING TO HEALING

Opening fully to love is your healing. Your physical healing to the greatest possible extent is your body's opening fully to love.

Healing energy is love. Your divine love for your children is healing for them but it is also healing for you. The most loving gift you can give your children is to open to your own healing source. That is the only part of you that has what you want to give them. If you do not receive it into your own body, if you try to make it somehow bypass you to get to them, you miss the point. Loving yourself is loving others, just as loving others is loving yourself.

As you open to your wholeness and experience the power of love, your body seems less significant to you; it does not dominate your consciousness. Paradoxically, it heals more easily, because love is the healer. When you focus on your body negatively, it becomes burdened and pressured.

When you generate an atmosphere of healing, what your body does step by step to heal will be what it needs to be. Some days things will look better, some days worse, but it is all part of the process.

Healing does not come from a bottle, although there are substances that are useful to support healing. Healing is a force. You are the healing force.

## DOING THE WORK

You do not have to believe. All you need is to do the work. You will get better at doing the work as you practice. The work is easy—the work of allowing—but you do have to devote yourself to it.

*How much time?*

Only twenty-four hours a day! But how much conscious time? As much as you can. The more time you give to it, the better. When you are doing enough consciously, you will establish a momentum that moves your progress forward without your having to push it continually. If you notice that the ball has stopped rolling, so to speak, you know you need to put in more time. It would probably be quite helpful if, while resting in bed, you invested five or ten minutes every hour in affirmations, visualization, meditation, inspirational reading and listening, and so forth. Ask yourself what would be the highest healing gift you could give yourself at any given moment. You do not need to establish a rigid regimen. Make it fun and creative.

The more work you do, the quicker your progress will be. If you do not believe in it fully, just see it as an experiment—you have nothing to lose. If you are successful, you can even believe, in the end, that medical science cured you—it does not matter what you believe cured you.

You could not be present unless there was power present. It required a great deal of power to bring your body and consciousness into form. There is power present simply because you are present. You are learning to open more fully to your positive power as a creator. It took you a while to create your present condition. It will not necessarily take a long time to create a new condition but it will take some time. Healing always begins where you are. If right now you are in a weak state, you start healing there. It may take longer than if you were in a healthier state, but the point is that you start now.

The most important factor in your healing is changing the beliefs that caused your present condition. These include the belief that you do not deserve healing, that you must be suffering because you deserve to be, that you have to be punished, and so forth. If you notice when you are coming from those beliefs, you can begin to change them. It does not take faith to change them—they do not make any sense to begin with; they are not logical. You simply need to see them clearly and assert the truth.

Ultimately, you do not even have to trust the healing force. All you need to do is to deliberately get out of its way. Although you do not need to trust it, you need to not distrust it. You can be neutral about it. You can take the attitude that you do not know if it will work, as long as you let it be there. Distrust is active—it stops the flow. Likewise, a lack of belief is not a problem if you do not actively disbelieve. It is a matter of being open, not to something foreign but to what is.

Discerning energies is not the point. As you listen for them, your discernment will grow. You are experiencing them whether you fully recognize them or not. Lack of discernment is not a major stumbling block. You open when you simply hold the intent to open. You can only do that in the present moment. Simply affirm, "Right now, I open," and feel yourself being quiet and receptive. If nothing else, concentrate on your breathing, and just keep feeling open. This is not really difficult. Even though it requires focus, it is a natural and easy process.

The only escape is through opening. You might think that death is an escape, but it is not. You would have to deal with the same issues even if you were free of your body. True, you would not have your body's pain, but your body to some degree is reflecting your consciousness, and you carry your consciousness with you. If you do not learn to open, you will likely recreate your pain in a future lifetime. So it behooves you to learn to open.

As long as you take action only in response to crises, you are supporting the belief that nothing is done until there is a crisis, which, of course, encourages crises to occur. Instead, we recommend that you take initiative to plan a program to deliberately build health. The medical approach is reactive; the holistic approach is active, taking the steps to create the reality you wish to create.

There are many ways of dealing with issues. When you

deal with them unconsciously, it is usually a slower process than facing them head-on. Sometimes people spend a lifetime dealing with issues unconsciously, occasionally while institutionalized. Their brains may not be consciously operating at all, but they are still processing their issues.

The lack of willingness to work consciously on one's issues is largely the reason people grow through pain instead of joy. Some people resist dealing with their issues at all, even if that kills them. There has to be willingness in order to process them. Commonly, people do not learn until not learning becomes too painful. They wait to be forced into dealing with their issues. You can avoid many problems if you deliberately open and do what you know you need to do before you reach that point.

When you are retraining yourself to live from your wellspring, at first it feels more like a discipline than something natural. In truth, you are already there, but you must pretend you are there until you can consciously experience it. The more you relax, trust, let go, and be in the present moment, the more you sense and align with it, until you wake up one morning and realize that you are there. You back into it, so to speak. You cannot move forward into it because it is not in front of you—it is within you. It is natural to experience being in your wellspring, and unnatural (although common) to experience being out of it.

**EXERCISE**

Bring a caressing quality of self-healing to all the parts of your body, one part at a time. It is probably not wise to start where you have pain, because it will tend to distract your concentration. When most of your body feels caressed and warm, include the parts of your body in pain. Finally, feel yourself caressing your whole body at once.

## LEVELS OF SELF

When one part of you experiences healing, it helps the other parts heal. If your body is strengthened through more appropriate diet, for instance, it can encourage healing in your emotions. One reason is that when your body is stronger, it is less of a drain on your energy. Therefore, you can more easily bring emotional issues to the fore and work on them.

When your physical body is weak or in distress, it tends to affect most your emotional body, which is closest to it. If your emotional body becomes distressed, it can affect your intellectual body, making it more difficult to keep your thoughts aligned with your true purpose. That can dissipate the energy of your spiritual, or innermost, body. Healing offered to any level of yourself can be beneficial and can help reverse this downward momentum, but working directly with your spiritual body can be especially helpful. Your spiritual body connects you with your essence. The more your spiritual body is developed, the more you can receive your essence's healing power. That can have a trickle down effect, helping your intellect become clearer, your emotions calmer, and your body stronger. Your spiritual body is your most general yet most significant influence in your life.

If you hold clear thoughts, your emotions will be able to respond above themselves to these clear thoughts, rather than being dragged down so much by the weakness of your body. That will help you strengthen your body.

## TRUST

If it were such an easy thing for you to trust fully your healing power, you would probably not be sick to begin with. So this is an important issue for you.

Letting go of your anxieties about your health can help you actually have the health you desire. However, it takes trust—not trusting something outside of you but trusting yourself and the universe, of which you are part. When you feel that you have to control everything in your life, that it has to be thus-and-so for you to feel safe, it is because you have not yet developed trust in the universe, or what some people call "God." Whatever you call it, it is a knowledge that the universe is beneficent, that no matter what the temporary appearance may be, there is a basic goodness to life, and that things work according to a process you can trust. That is the trust that will allow you to stop clutching. You live in a universe full of healing power. Your task is to open to it. When you do, it brings healing.

When you look at your children, you can see the fundamental goodness of the universe. Children bring issues into the world with them, so they are not necessarily completely open to life, but they do not have very well-developed intellects to get in their way so much, which is why they are so radiant. You can rest in the goodness of the universe. Assume that it will take care of you. That does require deliberate action on your part—it is not passive—but it does not require forcing anything. It is choosing what is natural. It is choosing to go with the flow of energy instead of against it. It is choosing to focus your attention on cause rather than effect. The cause of healing is this universal goodness. Your symptoms are sometimes effects of your lack of trust in that goodness.

Focusing on what is not there only robs you of precious time you could be using to focus on what could be there if you open to it. Those who recover from a life-threatening disease are often blessed for the rest of their life by what they learned during it. In many tribes, those who aspire to be leaders must go into the wilderness on their own and meet a challenge. They come back from that challenge capable of doing what they came on earth to do. We do not underestimate the challenge of physical pain and the specter of death—it is perhaps the biggest challenge a person could have. If you are able to trust in the face of this most difficult challenge, you will have the lesson of trust down pat. It will be something that can never be taken from you.

During this illness, you have been pulled along by effects rather than firmly coming into the place of cause. Affirmations are one way to come deliberately into a place of cause, because in an affirmation you are stating what you wish to cause. Be careful that you do not become wrapped up in what you do not want. If you are coming from fear, you will be causing from a negative place. Rather than affirming "I do not want to die," instead affirm "I choose to live." Embrace life rather than running from death. This is a very significant distinction: come not from desperation but from the knowledge of healing power.

## LETTING GO

There are two parts of healing. One is letting go of the old, and the other is bringing in the new. You cannot bring in too much of the new until you dispose of what is in the way.

What would happen if you let go? Or, what is the worst thing that could happen if you let go? Answering this can help you see what is in your way.

Sometimes people losing weight find that the last five pounds are the most difficult. Similarly, the last letting-go can be the toughest.

We are not suggesting that you *do* something, but that you simply allow what is normal to occur. When you cut your skin, for example, the natural, normal thing is for it to heal, but you have to stop cutting it. You are "cutting" yourself with some harmful beliefs. By letting go of them, you are simply getting out of your own way so that healing can occur. That takes deliberate action, but it does not involve forcing anything, trying, or struggling. It takes being mindful—noticing what you are doing—so that when what you are doing is not beneficial, you can allow yourself to be in a more natural, open way. Nothing in nature is tight or closed down. A plant never stops the flow of life force in it. It has no intellect that can choose to shut down. Human beings are blessed with the capacity to make choices. You can choose to shut down but you can also choose to open. If you had deeply made that choice in the past, opening would be automatic, but when you are changing a choice, it takes practice and time to reinforce it.

There are some things you cannot control, but you can always control how you respond to what is happening. You can respond by opening to your source or by shutting down. Opening to your source is very powerful—it can heal you. However, it requires letting go of the need to be in control of what is happening. Letting go is not the same as giving up. The fact is that no one can fully control everything in her life. Although you are constantly making choices that help create your reality, you also live with what comes as a result of your past choices and the choices of others.

Love is cause. True control comes from the power of love. You are more powerful when you open to love, less powerful when you try to control the manifestation of events. Loving changes events, but struggling to change events does not really work.

Your intent is something you always have control over. You may not always feel positive, but you can always hold a healing intent.

It is ironic that the more worried and anxious you are, the more you tend to try to control what you cannot, wasting the very energy you need for healing. Worry and anxiety can create a self-fulfilling prophecy.

Naturally, you desire to be as healthy as possible so that you can provide as much as you can for those you love and who count on you. Nevertheless, if you worry about that, you take energy away from building health. Therefore, what you worry about is more likely to come to pass. Your concern springs from love, but when it manifests as worry, it is mixed with fear and guilt. If you let go of worrying about things you cannot do anything about, and instead put your energy into simply being the love that is your reality, you hasten healing. That allows you to provide more for those you love.

When you don't hold onto anything, you have access to all things. This allows your situation to work out in the highest possible way.

The body is focused on survival, and is accustomed to using fear to protect itself. If you did not feel some fear during invasive medical procedures, that would indicate something wrong. What works better, though, is yielding. It is not easy to completely yield under such circumstances, but do the best you can. Afterward, you can release any fear you are still holding so that your healing can accelerate.

The more you experience and release your feelings, the more energy you have for healing. Blocked feelings withhold energy from your life. Fully experiencing your feelings is different from your mind racing about your feelings.

You actually have a lot of freedom right now. In particular, you have the freedom to open, a very important freedom.

Being free is not being without fear, but being okay with it. Being free is being okay with anything as it is.

Breathing is taking in life. Most people can benefit from being reminded to breathe. Someone quite ill may not be able to breathe deeply, but he can breathe freely instead of holding his breath.

If you were to breathe deeply and freely on a consistent basis, your healing would happen faster. You cannot breathe freely and hold on in other ways at the same time.

## YOU ALREADY HAVE THE POWER

We are not giving you anything you do not already have. In *The Wizard of Oz*, Dorothy already had the power to go home, but she did not know it until she went through all her drama; then it happened easily. You have always had the power to heal yourself, but you have not known it. Now you are starting to wake up. Rather than thinking of yourself as a victim of forces beyond your control, you are starting to realize that you have the healing power your body seeks. In fact, you *are* the healing power your body seeks.

## 25 • RAISING YOUR VIBRATION

A fever raises the body's temperature, burning away anything that cannot exist in that higher temperature. Spiritual healing raises the quality and quantity of the body's energy, burning away anything that cannot exist in that higher energy. Diseases, like everything else, have both a physical and an energetic component. If you raise the body's vibration to the point where the energetic component of a disease cannot exist, its physical component may also be eliminated.

   The consciousness of some diseases is particularly dense. Eliminating them requires sustaining a great intensity of energy. Many people are not capable of this. The body must be gradually conditioned to receive increasing amounts of energy. Without dedication and understanding, a person will not do what is required to raise his vibration sufficiently to heal a serious disease. However, everyone can raise his vibration at least somewhat by keeping as loving an attitude as possible. Nonintrusive, holistic approaches can also help raise your vibration and give your body what it needs to heal physically. Emotional and psychological healing and release are often crucial to raising your vibration. Spiritual practices that work directly with raising your vibration can be especially helpful. These include meditation, contemplation, chanting, and receiving energy from others—through a channel or healer, for instance.

   At the same time, anything you do can be used to raise your vibration—it is primarily a matter of the consciousness with which you do it. The more you spiritualize yourself through what you do every day, the more you will be capable of handling an intensity of vibration that can burn away what causes disease.

*Perhaps AIDS arrived on the scene as a sexual disease because of a misuse of sex. If we could raise that vibration, it would destroy the AIDS virus.*

AIDS has little to do with sexuality except that sexuality is a way to transmit the virus from the blood of one person to another. It is also transmitted through the needles of drug users, which is unrelated to sex.

Those with AIDS do not have it because of a misuse of their sexuality. The misuse of sexuality can contribute to a general lowering of one's vibration, but the misuse of anything in life contributes to a lowering of one's vibration. Raising your vibration through everything you do is a goal of the spiritual path.

## 26 • WELL-BEING IS YOUR BIRTHRIGHT

Sometimes people believe that it is not right to feel good about being alive while others are suffering. They limit their well-being because they would feel guilty, or to avoid a negative reaction from those who might resent it.

If you believe there is only so much well-being to go around, it may seem like an act of integrity to diminish your own so that there is more for others. In fact, well-being is a natural state available to everyone. There is an infinite supply.

It is commonly believed that everyone has to have his share of misery and suffering. Some people are thought to have more than their share and some, less. What would be a proper share of misery and suffering? Is there a set amount of it? Does everyone have to take some so that others will not have to carry too much?

It's true that every person has difficulties; otherwise, there would be little growth. How they are experienced, though, depends on the consciousness of the individual. It is possible to maintain well-being while meeting difficult challenges.

Well-being is your birthright. You do not need to let anyone or any situation take it from you. The more well-being you have, the more healing you can offer to others and to the world.

**EXERCISE**

Ask yourself what false belief most blocks you from having greater well-being. Record and explore the first answer that comes to mind.

Ask yourself whether you believe you have the right to well-being. If the answer is no, you might want to explore and change that belief. Believing you have the right to it is a prerequisite for having it.

## 27 • THE FLOW OF HEALING

When you send healing energy to others, you receive more yourself because it's flowing through you. You create a draft that draws more in and activates healing energy that was dormant within you. More than just receiving, the flow is what feels good.

Health requires a free flow of both giving and receiving. If you give and do not receive, you deplete. If you receive and do not give, you implode. Ideally, giving and receiving are in balance, allowing for radiance. Some people are blocked more in giving, some in receiving, and some are blocked in both.

For example, some people prefer giving because they feel more in control when they give, whereas they feel vulnerable when they receive.

False personality (ego) cannot give or receive energy. It is merely armor. There are people who do a lot for others but are not radiating much energy. If someone complains, "I give and give and give, and what do I get?" that is his armor speaking. Only essence can love and therefore heal.

Some people block receiving because they think they don't deserve it. Often when children are disciplined, their behavior is linked to their worth as a person. "I deserve" is a good affirmation—just those two words. You don't have to put anything after it. You deserve by reason of being; you don't have to earn deservingness.

Others block receiving because they feel it obligates them. They "keep score."

On the other hand, those who are selfish have a sense of entitlement, which is different from deservingness, and need to learn how to give in order to experience flow. Their receiving is low grade because there is not room for much to come in. When you receive freely, your "cup runneth over" and you have a natural desire to give. If your giving is blocked, whatever you receive tends to dissipate.

You are the center of a web that extends to many people: to your loved ones, through them to their loved ones, and so forth. When you let the energy of your essence freely radiate through this web, you help heal not only yourself but the world.

# BACK MATTER

# ABOUT THE AUTHOR

SHEPHERD HOODWIN has been channeling since 1986. He also does intuitive readings, mediumship, past-life regression, healing, counseling, and channeling coaching (teaching others to channel). He has conducted workshops on the Michael teachings throughout the United States and Europe.

Shepherd is a graduate of the University of Oregon. He lives in Laguna Niguel, California.

## ABOUT THE AUTHOR

https://shepherdhoodwin.com

TWITTER:
@shepherdh
@EnlightenNitwit

FACEBOOK:
https://www.facebook.com/shepherd.hoodwin
https://www.facebook.com/shepherd.hoodwin.author/
https://www.facebook.com/JourneyOfYourSoul/
https://www.facebook.com/EnlightenmentforNitwits/

shepherdhoodwin@gmail.com

Summerjoy Press
99 Pearl
Laguna Niguel CA 92677-4818

# GLOSSARY

*Agape*: A state of unconditional love for everything. This is considered the highest goal.

**Astral plane**: Where we go between lifetimes and when we are finished with the physical plane.

**Causal plane**: The next plane after the astral. Michael's plane of creation.

**Essence**: Soul, or higher self, in distinction to the outer personality, or lower self.

**False personality**: False ego, the part of self motivated by fear.

**Physical plane**: The densest of the seven planes, where we presently reside.

**Soul**: Essence, or higher self, in distinction to the outer personality, or lower self.

**Tao**: The All That Is. Usually refers to the dimensionless ground of being rather than to its expression in the seven planes of creation of the manifest universe. Michael normally uses the word *Tao* in place of God (depending on the beliefs of those listening) because God is usually personified and tends to connote something hierarchical and judgmental. They sometimes also use the word *God* to signify the overall consciousness of the manifest universe.

# OTHER BOOKS BY SHEPHERD HOODWIN

Available at https://shepherdhoodwin.com/book/

## *All Is Choice*

Few realize how profound, multi-faceted, and far-reaching the concept of choice is in our spiritual growth. This short book explores topics such as what is and is not our right to choose, our power as creators and the limits of our reality creation, how consciousness expands, and much more.

## *Being in the World*

This insightful book explores practical spirituality. Topics include aging, karma, time, and religion.

## *Compassion for Evil*
*A Metaphysical View*

*Compassion for Evil* explores the nature of evil from the soul's point of view, and how we can skillfully deal with it as lightworkers.

## *Embracing What Is*
*Spiritual Keys to Happiness*

This book is an abridged version of *Happiness and the Michael Teachings*, without technical Michael teachings terminology. A free version is available at Smashwords.com.

## *Energy Literacy*
*How to Perceive and Take Charge of Your Spiritual Well-Being*

*Energy Literacy* is an introduction to how to perceive our energy field and release negativity. Topics include chakras, contracts, vows, cording, entities, implants, psychic attack, earthbound souls, soul retrieval, and more.

**Enlightenment for Nitwits**
*The Complete Guide*

This hilarious metaphysical/self-help humor collection will appeal to Oprah and Dave Barry fans as well as those with more esoteric interests. In a style reminiscent of comedian Steven Wright, it's full of wry one-liners along with longer, hilariously mind-bending pieces on a wide range of subjects, tied together by the idea of clueless humans trying to find enlightenment.

"I love *Enlightenment for Nitwits*! It is the funniest book I have read in several decades. If laughter leads to enlightenment, it will certainly do it. Nothing—thank God—is sacred in this delightful spoof on life in general."
—C. Norman Shealy, M.D., author of *Life Beyond 100*

**Growing Through Joy**

This thought-provoking book explores the nature of personal growth.

**Happiness and the Michael Teachings**
*Learning to Embrace What Is*

Happiness is the ultimate goal of every spiritual teaching. Here we explore several principles of what the Michael teachings refer to as growing through joy.

**Healing the Gut**
*A Crib Sheet for Eliminating SIBO*

# OTHER BOOKS BY SHEPHERD HOODWIN

This short book offers tips for those with digestive problems and related diseases, focusing on the Specific Carbohydrate Diet.

***Journey of Your Soul***
*A Channel Explores the Michael Teachings*

This is the most in-depth discussion of the Michael teachings to date. It may also be the first analytical study of channeling written by a channel. It has forewords by John Friedlander, co-author of *Psychic Psychology*, and Jon Klimo, author of *Channeling: Investigations on Receiving Information from Paranormal Sources*. Klimo writes, "*Journey of Your Soul* may well be the best (Michael) book of them all due to its clarity, thoroughness, and detail, and thanks to the fact that the author, an exceptionally clear-headed Michael channel himself, brings real integrity and authenticity to our understanding of Michael in particular and to the channeling process in general."

***Loving from Your Soul***
*Creating Powerful Relationships*

This inspiring, transformative book explores the nature of love itself as well as practical matters of relationships. One reader wrote, "There are phrases that are so inspiring that I wrote them down to refer to when I need them. I am looking forward to reading this book again and again."

***Meditations for Self-Discovery***
*Guided Journeys for Communicating with Your Inner Self*

This is a beautiful collection of forty-five vivid, often pastoral, guided imagery meditations channeled from Shepherd's essence. There are many meditation recordings available, but this is one of the first collections of meditations in book form that can be read to oneself or others. Teachers and group leaders would find it particularly useful.

**Unconditional Love in Politics**
*Or Have You Hugged a Republican/Democrat Today?*

Is unconditional love in politics an oxymoron? Thus far, it's been a rare commodity if it's ever been there. This book explores what you can do about it, as well as why both right and left have useful parts to play in our evolution, the factors that influence a person's tilt to the right or left, and what unconditional love might look like in this sphere.

**Why We're Attracted**
*Spiritual, Psychological and Physical Elements That Draw Us to Others*

Just why are we attracted to some people and not to others? This book explores a multitude of factors on three levels: spiritual, psychological, and physical. Topics include agreements, life path, soul chemistry, male/female energy ratio, celibacy, body-type attraction, sexual orientation, monogamy, and polyfidelity.

# REVIEWS

There is so much inspiration in this book. It is also so concise and to the point, like a crowbar that opens a lid on your hard-sealed beliefs.

I find *Opening to Healing* to be both practical and encouraging. I've gone back to it many times and I am energized each time by the sensible take on the process of healing and growing. It is very positive in its approach to healing either yourself or someone else. If we get out of our own way, healing will happen.

This book is applicable to nearly any type of healing situation, regardless of the background of the reader. It is useful for practitioners and patients of both traditional and alternative medicine. The material is easy to understand and apply to everyday life. It helps us realize that we are not alone in our struggles, whatever they may be, and that there are many different angles to solving whatever health issues may exist. It is not only useful in treating illness and staying healthy, but is also a great, new perspective on how to view life in general. I used several of the techniques in the book to help me through some hard times.

I found this to be an excellent read that was well worth the time. I have read many journals and books dealing with all aspects of physical and mental health, and this one ranks right up at the top of the list. A must read for anyone interested in their health.

I would recommend this book to anyone. I've heard a lot about the power of the mind over the body but here I gained a better understanding on why it works. It has become my number one reference book on that topic.

This is a must read! It is a wise and patient vantage on the integration of spirit and matter.

I really enjoyed this book. It is filled with practical wisdom and is a refreshing take on healing. It has helped me understand how I can open to healing on my own life. I have found all the books in this series to speak so clearly to the core issues and to cut through the notion that "new age" material is fluffy—to me, it seems highly practical. There is a clarity and truth that rings out through the pages. (I also enjoyed the book *Loving from your Soul* by the same author.)

This book might just give you access to some tools for healing that you didn't know you already carried with you, and it does so in the gentlest of ways. A welcome antidote to the current age we live in.

This book reflected everything I was already processing but had no maps for navigating. I have grown a lot and could not be more grateful that there are people in the world who do work like this. This book is a masterpiece!!

*Opening to Healing* had me crying within five minutes, in the best possible way.

Superb!

Printed in Great Britain
by Amazon